Polygon Books

ISBN 0 904919 67 6

Copyright 1983
Allan Hunter and Mark Astaire

First published in 1983 by
Polygon Books,
1 Buccleuch Place,
Edinburgh.

Local Hero
The making of the film.

by Allan Hunter and Mark Astaire.

Cover and design by
Charles Miller

Typeset by
Edinburgh University Student Publications Board

Reproduced from copy supplied, printed and
bound in Scotland by
William Collins Sons and Co. Ltd., Glasgow.

LOCAL HERO

Written and directed by Bill Forsyth,
produced by David Puttnam

Introduction

The Spring 1982 issue of the film quarterly *Sight and Sound* regarded the latest statistics on British cinema attendances with alarm commenting that, 'the entire 1981 audience would have kept the cinema going for a mere three weeks during the long-distant boom year of 1946.' It is now obvious that the regular cinema-going habit in this country is becoming a thing of the past. The mass audience have chosen to view its entertainment in other forms: on television or video, in the comfort of their own homes without the possible drawbacks of sitting through inadequate presentation, finding a parking space, or hiring a babysitter.

The 1980s have given contradictory signals to the ever-ailing indigenous British film industry. On the one hand *Chariots of Fire* became the most financially successful 'foreign' film ever released in the all-important American market with a gross of 50 million dollars, and its unexpected Oscar win as the best film of 1981 was the first time the award had gone British since *Oliver* in 1968. *Chariots* was also seen as a spearhead for quality British film-making, and was one of a group of commercial and critical homegrown hits like *Time Bandits, The Long Good Friday, Gregory's Girl* and the Agatha Christie series. Conversely, 1981 was the worst ever year for home production and cinema admissions, with 1982 certain to represent a further considerable drop in the latter.

1982 saw the arrival of a fourth national television channel, and the announcement of ambitious plans for cable television in the not too distant future, further

rivals for the viewing public's attention. Realists within the business viewed it as a period of transition, there are still outlets for films, as television viewing figures show, and cable television has the potential to provide dozens more channels hungry for product. The audience is still there, but unless it is something very special the film-maker will have to come into the home instead of expecting the viewer to come to his showroom — the cinema.

It may well prove significant that Channel 4 provided a substantial injection of funding into the independent sector, commissioning films and guaranteeing the existence of *Moonlighting, Angel, The Draughtsman's Contract, Giro City* and the likes, and their appearance on both small and large screens. This latter development, combined with an extensive use of British expertise and studio space as an international hitching post for big spending productions like the Bond films, *Krull, Revenge of the Jedi, Superman III* and *Yentl* gave 1982 a healthy glow. The future then appears one of a blossoming low-budget independent sector seeking its finance from a diverse number of sources — the 1982 feature *The Appointment* was funded by the National Coal Board Pension Fund. The declining cinema audience which will survive, seems destined to provide merely a sales point for a production's real revenue in ancillary markets, it does not warrant big budget, big star mid-Atlantic films — they are simply too costly a risk. *Gregory's Girl* covered a major share of its budget on the returns from two cities, Glasgow and Edinburgh, and, the Egyptian and American backers of *Chariots of*

Dee Hepburn and Gordon Sinclair in a scene from the award-winning Gregory's Girl (1980) written and directed by Bill Forsyth.

Ian Charleson and Cheryl Campbell, with Edinburgh's Arthur's Seat in the background, during Chariots of Fire (1981), winner of four Oscars including Best Picture for producer David Puttnam.

Fire took a gamble and won, enjoying the rarity of covering their costs within Britain (largely thanks to a lucrative television sale). The rewards of a mass audience only go to the very special, something that catches the emotions; thus people have rushed to share the communal fears, joys and tears of *E.T.*, and it is a similar level of audience involvement that producer David Puttnam seeks in his big screen projects.

Therefore, it is against the backdrop of an industry in transition peopled by film-makers committed to a cinema of quality, experiences and audience involvement, that the making of *Local Hero* has to be seen. The film combines the talents of two major figures within that industry; Bill Forsyth and David Puttnam, people whose work and opinions can shape that very industry. The importance of *Local Hero*, after all just one film among dozens, should not be overstated, but its progress and entrance into the public arena will be observed by money men, critics, the media and industry colleagues. The success or failure of a £3 million British feature will have an impact on film-making in Britain, and perhaps in Scotland, certainly on the career of Bill Forsyth, more vulnerable than almost anyone else involved, and on all the projections and prophecies on the future of the industry.

This book is a result of the time spent on location with the cast and crew of *Local Hero* in Scotland, as well as many subsidiary interviews. Its intention is to chronicle the making of one British film, following it through the period of production and capturing an impressionistic account of the working experience of all those involved.

Burt Lancaster as Lou, the faded mobster in Atlantic City (1980), a role which won him the British Academy Award as Best Actor.

The Story

Houston, Texas. At the epicentre of the multinational corporation Knox Oil and Gas, billionaire boss Felix Happer (Burt Lancaster) plans the latest development project, the siting of an oil-refinery around the remote Scottish coastal village of Ferness. Happer decides to send a company man to clinch the deal in person. The choice is MacIntyre (Peter Riegert) on the assumption that with a name like that he just has to be Scottish.

Mac is summoned to Happer's luxurious penthouse office and told to keep in personal contact, especially if there is any unusual activity in the skies of Ferness. Happer's major obsession is the constellations, shown by the planetarium in his office ceiling.

On arrival at Aberdeen Airport Mac is met by Knox's man on the spot Danny Oldsen (Peter Capaldi), and together they report to the research laboratories for a low-down on the refinery by Geddes (Rikki Fulton), and his beautiful assistant, oceanographer Marina (Jenny Seagrove). They journey on to Ferness, receiving a grudging early-morning welcome from hotel proprietors Gordon and Stella Urquhart (Denis Lawson and Jenny Black). Gordon is a man of many skills, he runs the hotel, serves in the bar, settles the village accounts and will be Ferness's chief negotiator in the Knox scheme. Mac explains how Knox will buy everything around the village and within a mile radius inland. Urquhart and the villagers can sense big money and decide to string along the American.

During the ensuing days of their stay Oldsen and Mac

begin to appreciate the special charms of the area. Mac, who describes himself as, 'really a Telex man', begins to collect shells, go for long walks and stops shaving. Oldsen discovers Marina swimming in the bay and their mutual attraction develops — she talks of the economic future in the seas, and he teaches her Japanese.

The negotiations are progressing amicably — the villagers seem set to make a lot of money and Mac will have closed another big deal for Knox. Arrangements will be settled on the night of the ceilidh; a celebrated event which attracts all the villagers, including the beachcomber Ben Knox (Fulton Mackay), and Russian trawler skipper Victor Pinochkin (Chris Rozycki).

The mutual satisfaction of the negotiations is abruptly interrupted by the discovery that Ferness beach historically belongs to Ben's family, and there are documents to prove it. Ben is more than willing to talk, but stubborn in his determination not to sell the beach.

Mac (Peter Riegert) and Danny (Peter Capaldi) stroll along the beach whilst settling into the gentler pace of life at Ferness village.

Ben (Fulton Mackay) proves a stumbling block to the villagers' negotiations and explains his family's ownership of the beach to Gordon (Denis Lawson) and Mac.

Knox Corporation boss Felix Happer (Burt Lancaster) arrives to take control of the Ferness deal prompted by the reports of Mac. Opposite: the assembled flotsam and jetsam that comprises Ben's shack.

The ceilidh proves a happy, drunken occasion and Mac is enraptured by the appearance of the Northern Lights, a spectacular Aurora Borealis. He telephones Happer and enthusiastically details all he witnesses. Happer leaves for Ferness, lured by the visions of colour and comet showers and harangued by his demented analyst who has taken to making obscene phonecalls, and dangling outside his window.

Happer arrives to personally persuade Ben, but he too is charmed by the seas and skies of Ferness. He seeks a change of plan and Oldsen suggests a marine research institute perhaps called the Happer Foundation. Happer agrees and is fired with enthusiasm for the notion. Oldsen rushes to tell Marina the good news.

Mac is sent back to Houston, clean shaven and smartly-dressed to resume big city living. From the village he has retained the shells, photos of his friends and memories.

Danny contemplates the future of Ferness oil refinery or marine research institute, as Marina (Jenny Seagrove) reappears.

The cast (from the top) left to right: Burt Lancaster, Fulton Mackay, Peter Capaldi, Peter Riegert, Chris Rozycki, Denis Lawson and Jennifer Black.

The production

Viewing a finished film in the comfort of a cinema gives little evidence to suggest the tremendous amount of work that has gone into what is up on the screen, and rightly so. The illusory quality of cinema, of suspending disbelief has gone right out of the window the moment any audience starts to consider the sweat and toil that has gone into their entertainment. However, the making of any film involves a certain number of basic processes from writing a script to finding the money and choosing the cast. It can be a long haul employing the skills of a dedicated team; from the unseen hand of clapperboard boy, to the above the line attractions of the star. There are no set rules on how a film should be made and, as in all processes leading towards an end product, people are at work and there is almost a factory line through which the film must pass. There is also uncertainty, hopes and dreams and nobody is really assured of the outcome until critics and public have sat in judgement. A project like Richard Attenborough's *Gandhi* became a twenty year obsession for its maker, whilst Jerzy Skolimowski's *Moonlighting* represents the other extreme, having been written, shot and premiered within six months. *Local Hero* is more representative of the norm with its premiere in the Spring of 1983 representing the culmination of three and a half years of thought, preparation and hard work.

Producer David Puttnam set the ball rolling in 1979 with an idea for a comedy he wanted to make, as he recalled, "After the showing of *That Sinking Feeling* at the Edinburgh Film Festival in 1979, I talked to Colin Young about a certain type of film that I wanted to do, Colin had seen the film and he said he thought I should see it. Bill then came down to London and showed it to me and gave me a script of *Gregory's Girl*. I felt that *Gregory's Girl* was the same thing again to an extent,

and even if it wasn't the same thing again it didn't represent a major breakthrough for him, this was my feeling, and it certainly didn't represent any kind of major breakthrough for me because it was a rites of passage film, and I felt that I'd done a rites of passage film with *That'll Be The Day*. So, I said that I didn't want to do *Gregory's Girl*, but I'd love to commission a screenplay from him on a different area. I sent him some press cuttings I'd dug out about oil in Scotland and about a particular story, we gave some money to a journalist to research further and to follow up these same stories and Bill sat down and wrote a two page treatment. He got the go-ahead on a two page treatment to commission a screenplay." Forsyth gives Puttnam all the credit for providing the original idea for the film, its raw material, which he claims only to have moulded into something more reflective and away from an undesirable element of technology associated with the oil business. "David phoned me up one night and asked me what I was doing on Wednesday night and I said nothing, so he said I will see you at BAFTA at 7. I went down to BAFTA. He had hired a theatre and he showed me *Whisky Galore,* we didn't say anything, we just sat in the theatre and watched it. At the end we said that's very good and all that, and went our separate ways. That way he planted the seed; and over the next couple of weeks, I was living down in London, cutting *Gregory's Girl* and he was just finishing *Chariots of Fire*, so we were both hanging around Soho and bumping into each other. That's really how it started. He really initiated the idea with *Whisky*

Early on during the production Bill Forsyth and first assistant-director Jonathan Benson (left) work out a scene with two genuine Houston policemen enlisted for the filming.

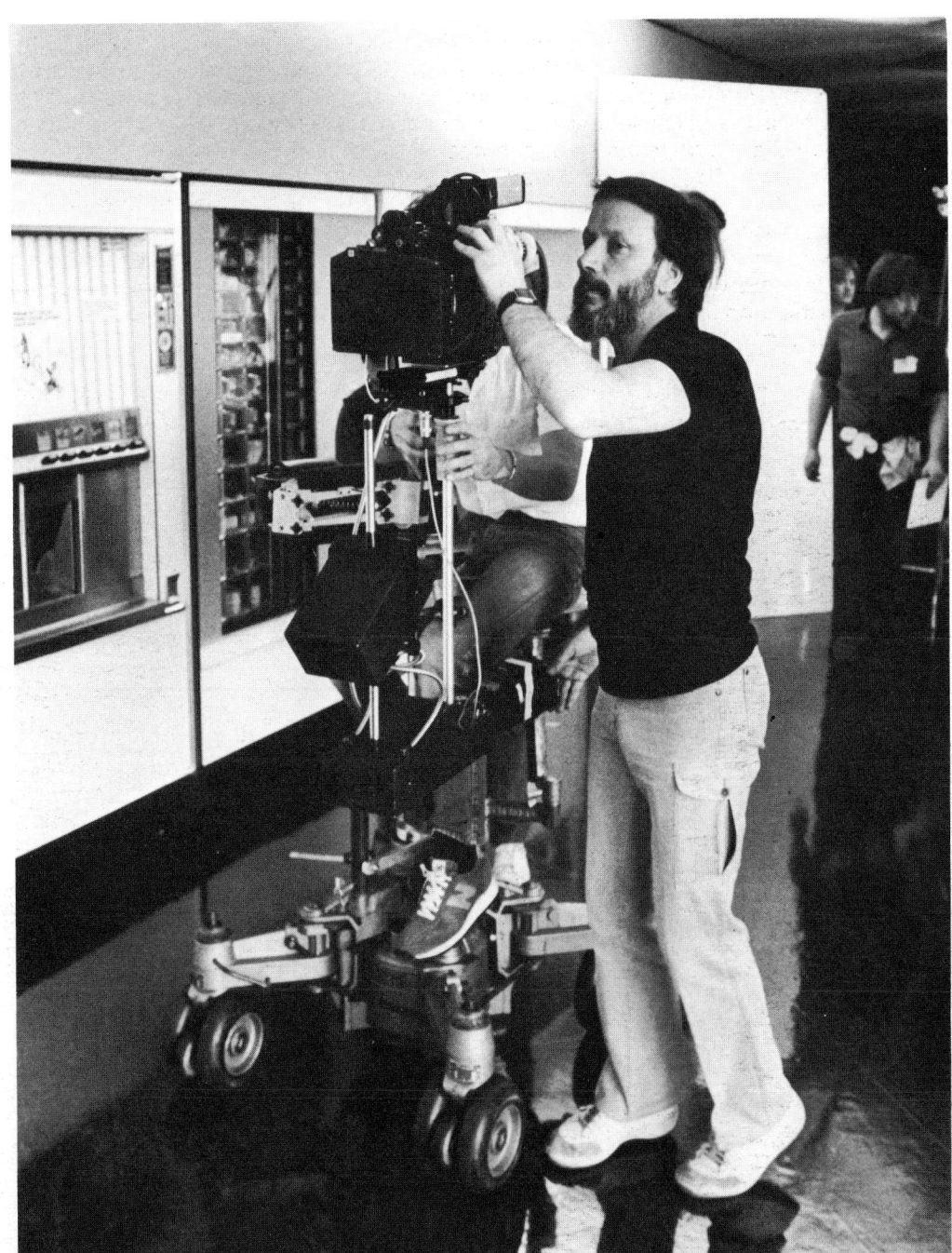

Lighting cameraman Chris Menges lines up a shot during the time in Houston.

Bill Forsyth, dressed for the variable Scottish weather, checks out a scene through his viewfinder.

Galore, which dealt with a small Scottish community and some eccentric event happening inside it, that was the basis of it. Because the oil thing is quite prominent the modern equivalent would be the oil industry. The only direction I pointed it in initially was to get it away from the idea of oil rigs and the hardware of the business, something I wasn't interested in. The first thing I decided was that there would not be an oil rig in it, or if it was it would be in some eccentric way, as in the documentary at the start of the film, or a model. That was in September 1980. It was not until March-April '81 that I had time to sit down and write it. I wrote it between May '81 and September '81. So, within a year of David making the initial approach to me, we had the script. That's quite short, it normally takes longer to put a film together."

It's during the scriptwriting period that many of the other intermingled aspects of making a film start moving into first gear. Whilst writing, Forsyth began to picture locations, work out elements of the crew and mentally cast some of the parts, and Puttnam began to tackle the crucial area of finance. One of the frustrations he has continually voiced as a producer has been that, despite unrivalled British talents in all parts of the technical and acting fields, film-making here is thwarted by the lack of clear channels of finance. The bigger film companies shy away from backing British, and others refuse to take gambles. He was turned down by many such companies for *Chariots of Fire*, before receiving backing from Egyptian and American sources. Despite all his success and high reputation, the situation appeared unchanged when he went cap in hand to find the money for *Local*

Bill Forsyth handles a complicated boardroom shot in Houston for his first big-budget film, backed up by Jonathan Benson, Anne Rapp, Jan Pester and Mike Coulter.

A short break in filming captures the Houston skyline. Set designer Roger Murray Leach sought a sense of isolation to capture the wealth and power of Texas.

Hero. "Goldcrest had put up the development money for *Chariots of Fire* and they didn't put up the production money because they didn't have it to offer. I think they wish they had and regret they didn't. Anyway they put up the development money for *Local Hero* which was turned down by Warner Brothers both as a treatment and as a screenplay. From very early on, as soon as they got the screenplay, Goldcrest offered to put up half the money for the film. I then schlepped around and failed, I was turned down by everybody that we went to, by EMI, by Warners and so on. Then on the evening of the British Academy Awards when Bill got his Best Writer thing James Lee, Chairman of Goldcrest, turned around and said look let's stop fucking about, we'll put up all the money, let's make the film and worry about it afterwards." The boldness of Goldcrest, part of the Pearson-Longman group and 60% backer of Richard Attenborough's 20 million dollar *Gandhi*, gave Puttnam his first wholly British financed feature for several years and a group of people with whom he was happy to do business. "Goldcrest have put together a really first rate management team and that's something that's been lacking in the film industry ever since I've been in it. For the first time in many, many years I'm dealing with professionals — people who are sophisticated not only financially but also in business." Goldcrest's faith paid off fairly quickly once filming began; three weeks into shooting Puttnam was able to make a deal with Warner Brothers for the North American distribution which effectively covered half the budget, in essence giving him what he had sought for several months beforehand.

During the pre-production period on a film the creative people begin to find out what is achievable in bringing something out of the realms of their imagination and into reality. Any production company must balance between the ideal and what is possible within the limits of a sensible budget. Associate producer Iain Smith was particularly aware of this aspect when scouting locations: "I think there is a possible financial and artistic conflict which Bill must feel. As the writer-director he is wearing two hats, and as the director he has to be aware of what is possible in translating the writer's work to the screen. At first the ideal location was on the Isle of Lewis, but it was 32 miles from Stornoway so for economic and logistical reasons it had to be decided this was out of the realm of possibility." Even the final locations which were chosen in Scotland and America proved something of a compromise as Smith explained: "We were looking for a beach that fitted the fantasy of Scotland which Bill had, but which just doesn't exist. We spent months looking for it. It was the same in Texas, we looked at Dallas before deciding on Houston and again there wasn't anywhere that fitted the fantasy that Bill had. That was one of the reasons we had to build an interior of Happer's office in a whisky distillery just down the road from our base in Fort William. Originally when I was on it we were to have more time in Texas. The problems of split locations in Scotland, Banffshire and Fort William, are quite a nuisance in terms of filming because of the problem of continuity with extras, moving equipment, having to remember which way to walk, watching out for shots of

Checking tides and lighting Bill Forsyth works on a scene at Camusdarach beach.

Happer finally gives vent to his pent up rage at the continual taunts and obscene messages from Moritz (Norman Chancer).

the beach so as not to see parts of the village and vice versa in Pennan." The need to find Bill's ideal setting of a coastal village with a harbour and beautiful beach adjacent was overcome by filming the beach sequences near Mallaig, and the village scenes at Pennan in Banffshire, resulting in the technical problems cited by Smith.

A further important feature of the time spent on pre-production is casting. Forsyth admits to placing a great emphasis on this aspect of his work, whilst Iain Smith commented: "Casting is very important. If you have the best actors then you can get away with being an inexperienced or bad director." The choice of actors and technicians on *Local Hero* was largely a happy one, if you select the best mix of professionalism and enthusiasm, then you can only hope that the confidence and care of those at the top percolates down. In the case of the actors Forsyth faced the alternating pressures of choosing 'names' for their own sake to attract potential backers, or the need to provide good reasons why unknowns are entrusted with major responsibilities. He admits to casting from the moment he begins writing the script and for him it had traditionally been an instinctive process. *Local Hero* was a little different in this respect as he illustrated with the case of Peter Capaldi, a young Glaswegian who makes his debut as the gauche Scot, Danny Oldsen. "In Peter's case there wasn't real resistance, I would have been quite happy to cast him just from knowing him, because of the mechanics of the industry we did screen test him and most of the characters, which turned out to be a good thing because it gave me a chance to work with them before filming

Burt Lancaster felt Bill Forsyth's script was the best he had read since Atlantic City, Fulton Mackay was less sure but has his fears allayed during filming in Scotland.

Chris Menges, a highly respected figure for his work with Ken Loach and on his own documentary East 103rd Street, brings his craftsmanship to bear on Local Hero.

With Peter Riegert are soundman Louis Kramer (left) and Mike Coulter who had both previously worked with Bill Forsyth on Gregory's Girl.

started. It would never have occurred to me to do screen tests, never. However, they actually turned out to be quite enjoyable." The evidence from *Gregory's Girl* highlighted Forsyth's talent to pick out faces and people, slotting them into representations of themselves not that far from reality. On *Local Hero* he shares the function with the casting director. "It's not as if I go around and sniff out everyone myself. This is where the casting director like Susie Figgis comes in. The first thing in good casting is finding a good casting director like Susie. We talked the same language and understood each other. When we met we tested each other out, I mentioned an actor and if she started laughing then I knew whether she thought it was a joke or not. We had a nice hour or two casting the film with people we didn't like and that was really good fun."

In the same way a cast is chosen, so the production and technical people are hand picked. *Local Hero* represents a blend of old and new, beginners and the very experienced. Forsyth has continued his association with Louis Kramer, the soundman on *Gregory's Girl*, and Michael Coulter, cameraman on the same production. Puttnam too has his pool of tried and tested talents including first-assistant director Jonathan Benson and fellow assistant Melvin Lind, who have contributed to *Chariots of Fire* and other Puttnam productions. Chris Menges, a much sought after figure within the industry and highly respected for his work with Ken Loach and on such features as *Angel,* was set for a key position as director of photography.

In the immediate period prior to the commencement of filming lesser but important tasks were completed, Lancaster flew in for wardrobe fittings and actors began to familiarise themselves with script and fellow performers during a period of rehearsals. Set designer Roger Murray Leach sees the bulk of his work completed before filming begins: "I'm just there to set the scene, to portray the character's personality in the physical surroundings. I help to create an environment in which the actors feel comfortable. I had a holiday in Houston in January and by mid February the three major locations had been established." The budget of £3 million, whilst a fortune compared to the £200,000 on *Gregory's Girl* or the £6,000 on *That Sinking Feeling*, is still modest by international standards and defines the limits of what Leach can do. "It's a small budget but all the money has gone on the screen, especially on the American side of the sets. We're trying to show great wealth doing exactly what it wants with the money. The setting is not exceptional for Houston, but I've never seen so much money in one city. We have saved on the Scottish end of the production to be able to create something that looks as if it belongs to a millionaire. The bulk of the design budget went into Happer's office. His penthouse has automatic doors, sliding panels and the ceiling opens into a planetarium. It's extremely hard to show enormous wealth. We tried for a sense of isolation, something big and fairly spartan. The office is surrounded by little rooms, he goes from the office straight into an outer-library, which will appear on the screen for only three to four seconds, but it is adding to the visual content."

Set designer Roger Murray Leach completes his main tasks before filming begins and can discover the seductive charms of Scotland along with the rest of the crew.

Clapperboard operator James Ainslie (right) calls the shots as filming begins with scene 1 take 1 in Houston.

Leach faced an additional problem, one to which any location film is laid bare, the vagaries of the weather. "The weather was dreadful, absolutely appalling, especially when we were trying to build the village church. The temperature was below zero and we had horizontal snow and winds so strong that people had to tie themselves to the scaffolding. The British and American split of locations was difficult because being thousands of miles apart it didn't matter which location I was in, because I felt I should be in the other one. We sailed a little close to the wind at times."

Leach was not alone in facing undesirable conditions, any film can expect problems to occur and still hope for the occasional blessing. On *Local Hero* it was the very welcome availability of Forsyth's choice Burt Lancaster, combined with fingers crossed weather reports which dictated the best period for the shooting of the film. "It was quite a tight thing for him," Forsyth said, "He had four weeks he could give us and we had to really schedule around these four weeks because he was involved with something else. It could have been disastrous if we had not got a good stretch of weather." Disastrous particularly for the budgeting of the film as Jonathan Benson, pointed out: "This is one of the most comfortable and accurate budgets I've known. If we'd had four weeks of rain then the budget would have been in trouble. The daily cost of Lancaster after contract was a lot — he probably cost as much for five days as I earn say in three years. The crew's wages are comparatively an inexpensive part of a budget; putting people up in hotels, providing food, servicing a crew, providing equipment that's what adds up."

Other problems stemmed less from the elements, more from man-made situations and thus solvable. At one point British Equity expressed their worry over the casting of Peter Riegert in the key role of Mac, voicing an understandable union-concern that the part could have been cast with an American-born but British resident member of our union. However, once persuaded of the need for Riegert all was well. More serious to the production was the inadequacy of the original location manager and as Puttnam ruefully recalled: "We had very few crises, in fact nearly all of them related, strangely enough, to the location manager. That cost us a good deal in money, time and trouble and I think that was almost the biggest problem we had during the shooting process." In this instance, the third assistant director David Brown took over the job, and Matthew Binns having completed work on Nicholas Roeg's *Eureka* (1983) flew in to fill the gap. A similar crisis arose when the original continuity person fell ill but was speedily covered for by the resourceful Pat Rambaut, as she explained: "I got a call on Thursday morning and came up from Glasgow to Fort William. I literally had a few days to prepare and I spent the Friday and Saturday in the hotel reading through the script. I usually have a week to sit in on rehearsals, go over the filming schedule and cross check the scene numbers. The process of continuity involves remembering when a character like Mac has a lot of change in his pocket, how unshaven he is meant to be and so on."

Five weeks before beginning filming Jonathan Benson joined the production in his role as assistant director. He described it thus: "I deal with everything

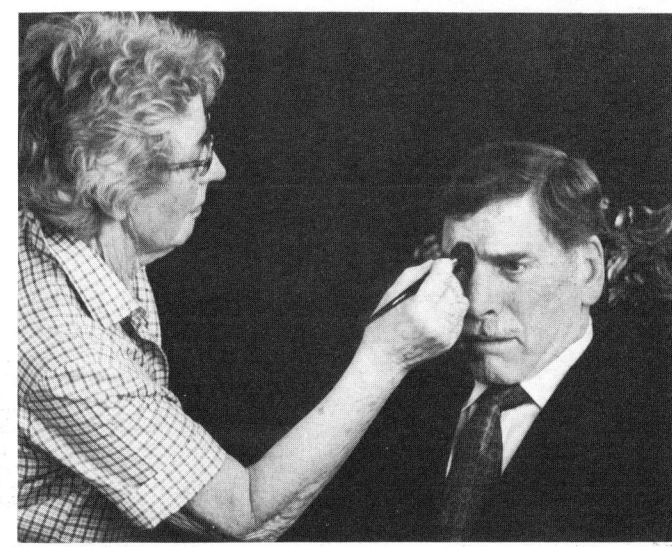

Make-up supervisor Tommie Manderson, with over four and a half decades of experience, strives for the natural look as she prepares Burt Lancaster.

Bill Forsyth wants shots that 'show care and humour' explains Chris Menges and the photo-crew set out to give just those qualities.

from the extras onwards, backing up the director by running the ship on the floor, shielding him from unnecessary distractions. It's mainly an administrative role with responsibility for extras, scouting locations, being *au fait* with the production and knowing all the problems. Actors need to feel they are not left out; they need encouragement like flowers, so it is vital to say that things went well, it's amazing how it helps. Man-management is important and I have a persona for dealing with large groups and making people think they are having a better time than they actually are." That proved less of a chore on *Local Hero*, everyone admitted to having a pretty good time.

Benson, a respected industry veteran with over 25 years experience, was the only assistant director to go with the production to Houston, where filming began on April 26th, 1982. Forsyth had entered the country prior to the rest of the crew, meeting press in selected cities where the dubbed version of *Gregory's Girl* was about to win perceptive reviews and heartening box-office returns. The American filming was squeezed into seven days, with a hard working schedule, as Benson remarked: "Filming in America was surprisingly similar to working here. Houston is not a centre of film-making so it was a bit like working with non-film people an amateur night to a certain small degree. They were hard working, nice people but we needed to teach them how to do certain things. We filmed in seven days what would normally take twelve, but there were no unions. However, people only work as long as they are rewarded. If we had worked at that pace all the time people would only have worked at half speed, as they physically lose interest." A working day lasting from 7 in the morning until 12 midnight was not an uncommon event during the time in Houston and serves well to illustrate the degree of commitment of those involved.

The unit finished in Texas and quickly returned to the vicissitudes of the Scottish climate and a schedule still tightly constructed around Lancaster's availability. Forsyth, however, proved a man sure enough of himself not to be rushed unnecessarily, expressing more concern over the finished film than temporary delays: "In any film no matter what the budget circumstances are film is not really a big expense. Once you are filming a scene film is such a small cost. The setting up of the scene is the cost, so it seems senseless to set up the scene and all that that involves and then come away without the scene worked out properly, when all you are spending is a few more quid on the film. It seems a lot to do 15 takes but then I always tell myself, it would be silly to walk away not being happy about it. So we just keep going. I don't think we went to any more than 20 and the budget for the film was 16 to 1, so theoretically we could shoot each scene 16 times. Most of them were five or six and just occasionally we went over ten. I think we were pretty well under budget for the film."

On the set Forsyth can often appear a lonely, isolated figure squelching through some newly rain-sodden terrain in blue woolly hat, green windcheater and bright red training shoes. An intensely shy man; he relies on Jonathan Benson to corral and command the extras, all locally recruited from press adverts, and even allows him to call action and cut on the less intimate scenes, the traditional preserve of the director. His relationship with the actors is that of a confidant, eschewing hierarchical distinctions, he remains open to suggestions, likes to develop scenes and never feels he should have to coax a performance from an actor. On a Forsyth film there is room for everyone to breath. An experimental tool of his trade on *Local Hero* was a video playback, which he later admitted as having been less than a roaring success, but which allowed him some opportunity to gauge the feel of a scene and provided a hidey-hole away from the crowds where he knows he will not be disturbed. At times Forsyth is more than appreciative of Benson's ebullience. "He was great and supported me. He said I can tell by what you are wearing how shy you are and how much I've got to do."

The bulk of the Scottish filming took place during May and June amongst the split locations of the beautiful beach at Camusdarach and the enchanting village of Pennan. Lancaster was the first of the principal players to complete his work and declared himself more than satisfied with the results, Forsyth commented: "I could make films with him forever." The remainder of the shooting, which at one point had been set for the King's Buildings area of Edinburgh University, was eventually completed in England during a week in early August. A late change in casting brought in much loved performer, Rikki Fulton, to replace fellow Scot Bill Patterson in the cameo part of the scientist Geddes.

Filming, with allowances for weather and tides, was

First assistant-director Jonathan Benson indulges in a little animal protection whilst filming in the village of Pennan.

generally a dawn to dusk business involving technicians setting a shot from 7 in the morning, caterers with a steady stream of hot-drinks and small culinary triumphs, performers going through make-up and wardrobe, the local extras, police called up to stop traffic disrupting a shot, and even the services of a nurse. The latter proved only too welcome for the many sufferers of travel sickness on the bumpy, twisting hour drive from hotel to location at Camusdarach.

The set of a film often appears unwelcoming as filming is a long process involving much standing about. However, this is only the impression of the non-participant, every member of a crew has a specific function and each is aware of their responsibilities, it is the level of absorption which can appear off-putting to the outsider.

Local Hero, as David Puttnam emphasises, is an attempt to, "take films back to where they started as a cottage industry, made by serious craftsmen," and when a cast and crew of such professionalism is assembled on one production, they can't help but engender great expectations. Jonathan Benson again, explains the atmosphere on the film. "Coming to work on the first day was exciting, with these recent award-winners all at the top of the business. One doesn't usually have that feeling, over the years the process can become a bit mechanical, and it's a huge bonus knowing one is working with people who are peaking in the business." The enthusiasm and application of all was visible, even someone with 45 years experience like make-up supervisor Tommie Manderson who could have been excused for having seen it all before, enthused about Puttnam and the production. "I read through the script and have three or four weeks to think about beards, moustaches and so on. Make-up happens in the hours before the first shot. I have to look out for lights gleaming on balding heads. I study faces to make them look like the characters. This is a modern production, gone are the days when everyone just plastered on make-up, now we're striving for a more natural look."

The natural look is one of the hallmarks of the production in its search for a deliberate unstylish appearance and made life considerably easier for wardrobe mistress Penny Rose. "My role starts about five or six weeks before filming begins. We had a budget of £15,000 (costumes coming mostly from Oxfam shops), compared with say £70,000 on *The Wall* (1982). There is really nothing special about the costumes in the film. The wardrobe of the extras is their own, apart from hats and scarves. This is quite an easy film to do, Lancaster coming over about five weeks before production for fittings, all his stuff being tailor-made, but I often find it harder to do ordinary people than something outrageous like *Quest for Fire* (1981)."

Chris Menges summed up the relationship between the director and the crew with his comments on his own role in the production. "As a cameraman you try and work with a conception of the photography, what does the story need and what does the director need. You try and give what they need, plus something that is a surprise, that's the normal way I work, with Bill it's different. Bill is not into photography *per se,* he wants more than that from his photocrew. He wants shots that show care and show humour, not shots that are pretty. If they are pretty it's because the script wants that, or if the script says, 'oyster catcher flying over the sea', then he saw that. My job was totally different to any other film; Forsyth doesn't want strong photography, he wants rather quiet amost subdued photography. What he wants from the cameraman is how will we make this funnier, how can you as the cameraman contribute. It doesn't have to humour *per se*, what becomes important is to give it care."

David Puttnam was equally aware of the attention and involvement necessary in his conception of a producer's role. "I think I have an influence over the pre-production process in terms of putting together a crew, the tone of the film, the mix of the crew, especially in a situation where Bill was taking certain people from *Gregory's Girl*, but a lot of the crew were new to Bill so I had more influence maybe than usual. I had the final O.K. on the main cast. Basically the shooting period of any production, if the producer has done his job properly in pre-production, is the easiest time for him. He's there to deal with crises if and when they arise, and if they don't arise your life is reasonably easy. On this film because we were blessed with basically very good weather and because we had an amiable cast, we had very few crises." The lack of such events gave Puttnam a comparatively easy shooting period, allowing him to reap the rewards of his work on *Chariots of Fire* with the visibly healthier British presence at the Cannes Film Festival and even, at times, leaving him rather redundant, as Scots actor Denis Lawson observed: "He said he got worried because there were not enough problems and he didn't have a job. In fact he has made problems because he got bored." Other actors observed that Puttnam's presence was only notable by its absence during filming, a fact he would regard as a compliment.

The remoteness of many of the Scottish locations caused some problems on the technical side however the enforced camaraderie of cast and crew reliant on each other for company and social intercourse quickly created a friendly atmosphere. Problems arose for Michael Bradsell, the film's editor who had worked with Puttnam previously on *That'll Be The Day* (1973) and *Stardust* (1974). Part of his work was carried out whilst filming continued in Banff and the facilities of the Banff Springs Hotel for projecting film were less than ideal. A small cubby-hole in the hotel with inadequate blackout and the difficulties in setting up projectors, made Bradsell's job more pressurised, but as the only alternative was Glasgow then it's make do or mend. However, the other exigencies of faraway Scottish locations provided more comic experiences. Edith Ruddick, one of the more elderly members of the company, recalled her special difficulties with the sanitation conditions at Camusdarach beach: "When we got there the girls' caravan, I'm loosely called a girl, had no plumbing arrangements connected to the water supply. I complained very loudly that I had been engaged as an actress, and not a camel. It was a terrible problem, if I had had a big part I'd have been driven frantic worrying. I needed to go to the loo all the time because the actual one, the proper one with plugs and

Peter Capaldi and Jenny Seagrove enjoy the glamour of filming; "blue nose, blue fingers and tatty hair!".

things and a flushing system in a hut was two fields away and in this lavish production by Enigma films you had to negotiate two fields with stiles, over barbed wire, through a menacing herd of sheep which I'm sure contained several of the vicious male types, through innumerable cowpats, holes which had been dug deliberately and that sort of thing. Being a very obedient kind of person I wore everything the wardrobe told me the old lady wore; my long tweed coat, my tweed skirt and my petticoat, blouse, cardigan and my thermal underwear. It made me lots of friends because I was always getting my coat or something stuck in barbed wire and always being released by all sorts of pleasant people."

Pleasant people weren't too hard to find in the proximity of the *Local Hero* unit, even the locally recruited extras put up with the long standing about and the many retakes with equanimity and enthusiasm, all for £9.50 a day. The younger extras had planned the spending of their earnings in advance, working towards a paddling pool, fishing rod or, appropriately enough, a first camera. Denis Lawson testified to the family atmosphere on the unit: "It's been wonderful, we've had some really joyous times. When we drove over from Fort William to Banff I wasn't really looking forward to the drive, it seemed rather a schlep, we were all a bit tired and had got a bit legless the night before. We were all in Mini-Metros, Jennifer Black in her car and then there was Charles Finch and the production secretary Teresa Colman. We did not set off together at all, but left at ten minute intervals or something like that, driving very slowly, it was the most glorious day and about half way across somehow we all caught up. We ended up going in this little convoy and then someone ran out of petrol. Usually when that happens I know I would get a bit

Members of the cast pose with local extras from the Fort William area during the shooting of the church scenes.

uptight, but at that time it was very funny. There were six of us there, none of us knew anything about cars and Teresa did not even know she had run out of petrol. We were all looking under the hood when she said I think the accelerator has gone. She was pressing the accelerator and I said it seems to be alright, and are you sure you haven't just run out of petrol. She had just half a tank when she left and we'd driven about a hundred miles, eventually we realised we had run out of petrol. Then we had to bargain for some petrol and came upon a Georgian house for lunch where we went for a swim afterwards, and spent three hours there and just toddled off. It was a kind of magical day, the whole social atmosphere has been like that." Roger Murray Leach illustrates the way the unit was infested with good spirits: "I never realised why the Victorians romanticised Scotland, what exactly they were on about, now I do. I've never worked with a group within which there has been less friction. People have become enmeshed in the atmosphere of locations, I think the magical effect on Mac in the script happened to the whole unit, we've been buying books on birds and flowers and collecting seashells."

Local Hero then was the original good time had by all despite the often extensive pressure on the unit. It was generally agreed that a too-lengthy script had restricted the amount of space available for Forsyth to improvise and encourage the spontaneous element of previous features, whilst an already over-rigid schedule had prevented the script being pruned more drastically. Another element of pressure arose with the wide media attention which the production received. Television documentary crews, journalists and writers were all eager for an inside story of the great Forsyth-Puttnam collaboration. Forsyth disliked all the attention, wary of being billed as more than he deserves and wide awake to the notion that if a lot of people are willing you to succeed, then an equal number would be just as happy to see you fall at the next hurdle. However, two big names of the British film industry can't help but attract a lot of interest. Every film employs a unit publicist to co-ordinate relations with the press and arrange interviews.

Jonathan Benson, the only assistant-director to go with the unit to America, with fellow assistant Matthew Binns who flew in from another production to work with David Puttnam again.

On *Local Hero* this was the function of former film-journalist Sue D'Arcy. Her work was virtually done for her and she readily admitted to never having seen anything like the level of interest shown with some representative of the media there nearly every day of filming.

The happiness of the filming was summed up by the party marking the end of the major location work where colleagues gathered to say goodbye to friends and recall the little moments from shooting; like Forsyth spontaneously sweeping the young actress Caroline Guthrie off her feet for her first ever helicopter ride, the sly corruption of the English crew by the Scots, or the newly minted Scots accent of the irrepressible Jonathan Benson, half a stone lighter than when filming began. As Peter Riegert said: "I think it's as good as it gets. Not just because it's been a lot of fun, and the people are great but the process has been great, Bill is great and it's been terrific."

The bulk of filming over the footage is then cut and dubbed into a working print ready for the music track and the publicity machine to prepare the finished product for release. These latter stages are centred around the Enigma offices in London and the technical facilities of EMI's Elstree studios in Borehamwood. The latter is an unprepossessing edifice, an uninspiring home for a thriving industry, and as Bill warned: "You don't want to eat here, the food's rubbish!" It is now that the talents of editor Michael Bradsell are called upon. "Firstly there is the problem of length, it is possible to work towards a certain time. Unless it's a blockbuster type film exhibitors don't like films longer than two hours, if it is two hours ten minutes or longer then it is not economic for them, and then again it really shouldn't be under 90 minutes, but that's rarely the problem. *Local Hero* could be rather a long film, it will never be a short one, I think about 110 minutes. I like to try and surprise the director. The content of the material dictates the style, when I cut the sequences together, I aim at a first cut immediately. When you are working in isolation it is, of course, rarely right as other scenes change the emphasis. It is a flexible process which goes on all the time." Bradsell's work involves a close collaboration with both Forsyth and Puttnam; the latter who, at this stage in the production is active in many areas, as he points out: "I work with him on the first cut, it's Bill's cut, but I have my own views, most important of all I am making sure that the film's birth is properly organised; to see the way that it's handled is right, the image it is given is correct, and that it's given a chance to live." This again raises a pet subject of Puttnam's — the British lack of technical capability to preview a film's fine cut to an audience in a normal cinema surrounding. "There is no normal theatre in Britain equipped to run a film in double-head projection, that's to say a cutting copy. You cannot do it. There are dozens in America, and they would never dream of finishing a film without previewing it and previewing it. I find that the most extraordinary thing and we are in the process of actually financing one, because it's not good running a film at BAFTA or at the Studios. You can't say we'll invite an ordinary audience, the instant you walk in there and sit down you're not in an ordinary theatre and you've already got an attitude." The problem on *Local Hero* was unsatisfactorily resolved with a public screening of a 'work in progress' at an Elstree Studio's dubbing theatre in early October. An advert in the local *Borehamwood Post* attempts to attract Puttnam's average audience.

Ideas on the publicity and promotion of the film have been planned, discarded and rethought right from the beginning of shooting and well into the winter the correct poster image is sought for the film's release.

Whilst the editing continued the soundtrack was completed by Mark Knopfler, most famous for his association with *Dire Straits,* and at the time of filming riding high in the British charts with a hit single *Private Investigations* and an equally successful album *Love Over Gold.* His casting can be credited to David Puttnam, not surprisingly considering the importance of music to his films. "I listen to a lot of music of all sorts and whenever I'm reading a screenplay it has a tonal quality in it, a musical quality and there were a few tracks on the album *Making Movies* that reminded me of the film and I also thought the film had a danger of being a bit too lyrical and needed a punch in it every now and then. Same thing as we had with *Chariots of Fire,* where the music was consciously selected before we ever shot the film to work against the period, rosy-glow sense of the picture. Quite deliberate. There were two temptations with this — bagpipe music or a sort of lyrical string quality music — because it is that kind of lyrical, if you like Capraesque film. Again, trying to work against that, trying to give it a contemporary feel, Mark's music was the sound I had. I played the stuff that I was talking about to Bill and he liked it enough to want to meet Mark." Forsyth was indeed impressed with Knopfler: "He wanted to write music for films, and his manager had written to, I think, six or ten producers. Only two wrote back and one of them was David. We met quite early on and he had already been offered a couple of films and turned them down. He was offered *Urban Cowboy* (1980) and he had a chance to work on *An Unsuitable Job For A Woman* (1981). So he was prepared to wait until the right thing came along. So we met and he read the script and said he was interested, I like his music and he was keen so that was that, really David's little bit of casting, Mark and I are quite similar people."

The public preview invited an audience to give a response to the film asking them to fill in a questionnaire saying how they rated the film on a scale of one to ten, their favourite scene, favourite character and so on. It is important for the production to gain this objective eye and also to be as ready as possible for public display. The film stood a genuine chance of becoming the Royal Film Performance of 1983, a prestige showcase for the production's launch but not an essential one. An understandably twitchy Puttnam can only have been heartened by the response of *Guardian* film critic Derek Malcolm, who whilst bemoaning the non-appearance of the film in the London Film Festival of November 1982, hailed it as the best representative of the new British cinema which would be seen that year. The prestige Puttnam feels essential to the film's ultimate success had already begun to accrue.

The making of *Local Hero* was a little different than the average production; enjoying a more convivial atmosphere than most, an air of confidence born of professionalism and ability, a sense of excitement and expectation heightened by the intense interest of the outside world and the chemistry of Forsyth and Puttnam. The film, whether a success or failure (and the latter can never be discounted) is important for other reasons as well; for the future of a quality British cinema, for the aspirations it may arouse within Scotland and especially for the career of Bill Forsyth. Puttnam believes the film will give confidence to Scots writers to tackle their issues in their own terms, but it was significant that many of the Scots on the film had no work lined up once filming was completed, whilst the English members of the team had an industry to which they would return.

Local Hero however, is Forsyth's film and he has appreciated both the comfort of the budget and the support of the large crew in pushing him and helping him to expand his creative talents on screen and continue to learn about the world of films off-screen. He will go on making films, he is a genuine and captivating talent who has a firm notion of his own worth. The making of the film as expressed through the respect and comments from his many colleagues and co-workers would probably cause him acute embarrassment and so the eloquence and feeling of what's on screen must stand as the best testament to what the man and the production are all about.

American continuity woman Anne Rapp, complete with detailed file of notes, clarifies a point with Bill Forsyth.

Over here
Burt Lancaster and Peter Riegert

In *Local Hero*, Bill Forsyth takes a giant step into the international film scene with a large crew, a substantial budget and professional Equity actors. The humour and action of his previous films have centred on Glasgow, but the evidence that his comic world has travelled well, as indicated by the success of *Gregory's Girl* in Europe and America, bodes well for the new film.

American actors Burt Lancaster and Peter Riegert take two of the key roles in the new production. What had attracted them to work with a relatively unknown commodity like Bill Forsyth in Scotland, hardly the centre of the film-making universe? Veteran Lancaster gave the best reason any actor can: "A good part in a good script. I had not seen any of his films; as a matter of fact I didn't meet Bill until I stopped in London for wardrobe fittings, which was also the day of the British film awards. It was the first time I'd met him but I'd read his script and know he's a very talented boy, it's as simple as that."

Lancaster, a movie star since his first film, *The Killers* in 1946, has always been amongst the most forward-looking actors of his generation; establishing his own production company in the fifties, stretching his horizons as an actor working with directors like Luchino Visconti in the sixties in Europe, whilst appreciating the need for appearances in blockbusters like *Airport* (1969) to remain a viable box-office attraction. An Oscar nominee for his roles in *From Here to Eternity* (1953), *Birdman of Alcatraz* (1962) and *Atlantic City* (1980) and winner for *Elmer Gantry* (1960), Lancaster 70 this year,

has enjoyed a highly successful career and an admirable range of parts. It was a largely unexploited dimension for comedy that Bill Forsyth sought to tap in casting Lancaster as Happer, the eccentric billionaire head of Knox Oil. "When I was writing the script I started to imagine him saying the words," Forsyth recalled: "I mentioned early on to David and everyone else, that I thought Lancaster would be good for it, and it was a real piece of good fortune that we got through all the stages successfully, like getting to him first of all and getting him to read the script, because I'm sure he gets so many scripts and does not read half of them anyway." However, as with all film productions there were other options pencilled in if the ideal casting of Lancaster was unobtainable, in this case Charlton Heston or Sterling Hayden. For the role of Mac, Happer's emissary to the Scottish village and the central figure of the film, Henry Winkler, star of the television series *Happy Days*, was a possibility before settling on the casting of Peter Riegert. Riegert's name appeared out of the blue during casting as he recalled: "As I understand it, there was this reporter Joan Goodman who I met five years ago, who happened to be in the office when they were talking about finding an American for this part, and she asked if they'd seen me, they said no, so she said they should."

Riegert, a native New Yorker and a graduate in English from the University of Buffalo, was employed as a social worker and teacher before entering the acting profession in the early 1970's. Ten years on he now has a substantial amount of stage and film work to his credit beginning in off-Broadway shows, before graduating to Broadway with a starring role in *Dance With Me*. His film work includes Joan Micklin Silver's *Head Over Heels* (1979) and *National Lampoon's Animal House* (1978). What then had attracted him to the gentle humour of *Local Hero*, a far cry from the raucousness of *Animal House*? "I think the script is excellent. Ironically when I read it, I'd got home very late in the morning, 5 or 5.30, and couldn't sleep so I picked up this huge script.

Mac, the company man, captured in his natural environment — on the telephone closing a deal.

Bill Forsyth sought to exploit a dimension for comedy within the Lancaster persona.

The scripts in Britain are about three inches longer than they are in the States. I got it in the afternoon and didn't want to have anything to do with it because it was so big. Anyway, I figured I'd read a couple of pages. Next thing I knew it was 7.30 in the morning. My first impression was, I am going to do this job, which is very rare."

In his preparation for the role Riegert spent some time in Houston, his character's main base for wheeler-dealing. Ironically it was there he saw *Gregory's Girl*. "I saw a part of it in Houston of all places and the audience was going crazy for it. They loved it. I would have thought Houston was the last place for that reaction, and at the end of the film when the kid holds up the sign for Caracas, the audience was laughing so hard that they couldn't hear the last kid speak. I wanted to say, Hey, I didn't do this one but I'm doing the new one, wait until you see the next one!"

Both of the American actors brought their professionalism to bear on the production. Lancaster, with an ease born of long experience, was able to help his fellow workers. Bill Forsyth recalled an incident early on in the Houston shooting which illustrates the last point: "I remember the first scene with Lancaster when he has to push through some policemen to get to his car. We had real cops, who were a bit timid of Lancaster. He was supposed to barge through and part them, and they backed off. I said to them to allow Burt to push through and went back to the camera where I saw him talking to them and I thought he's going to be O.K., he's helping out, he was just saying the same in American. He saw me seeing him do this and before he went back to his mark he came over to the camera and said, 'I hope you don't mind me talking to the other performers but I thought I could help.' I said he could do it whenever he liked." Once the initial awe of appearing with the legendary Burt Lancaster had worn off, he proved a valuable source of copybook cinema acting for others on the crew to observe at first hand. He was considerate too of the strain for newcomer Peter Capaldi, as was Riegert who shared many scenes with the young Glaswegian. "I met Peter in London the first day of rehearsal and as

Mac examines his souvenirs from Ferness and speculates on his friends and memories.

soon as I was introduced to him I thought he was perfect and we hit it off immediately. I felt I could use his inexperience to aid our relationship because he plays this naive sort of oil guy, and I play the American who is supposedly more knowledgeable."

The art of comedy is a fragile one at the best of times and the cultural clash of Americans and Scots might have been expected to endanger an understanding of Forsyth's comic universe. Such has not been the case on *Local Hero* as Riegert was quick to point out: "I find the Scottish people have a very similar sense of humour to mine, Bill used to tell me this all the time. He said you'll love Glasgow, it's just like New York. I think he meant the sense of humour, as Scotland's relationship to England is like New York's to the rest of America." Riegert perceives Forsyth as carrying on a great tradition in British film humour. "I grew up on all the Ealing comedies, Carry On movies and Ian Carmichael, Terry-Thomas, Peter Sellers. It was as much an influence as anything else in my life. I think the most wonderful contribution made by British movies is their love for people's eccentricities, and how the daily grind of the week or the day is filled with dramatic situations. Bill recognizes that real dramatic situations can be made out of going to the market for milk, when you've got a tack on your shoe." Lancaster too had been impressed by Forsyth's slyly humorous stance and found his broadly comic role a real challenge. "It's a very difficult role to play, as the character is sort of half mad. Forsyth is a very perceptive person about human nature and frailties, and in his view everybody is a little strange, but he treats it all very gently with a very light humour. When you try to play a character like this you don't know how far to take it, because it's meant to be humorous. You've got to be careful that you don't farcialise it, play it overboard, play it too big, which is the temptation, rather than let the total effect of what is happening effect an attitude of charm and mirth. You want to go in and

punch it up and that's very dangerous with his kind of writing. But it's really refreshing to find someone who writes with such a charming, lovely humour."

For both performers their first working experience of Scotland has been a pleasant one, a pleasure reflected in the concern they have shown over the production and their genuine interest in the other members of the cast and crew. Lancaster, a previous visitor to Scotland in pursuit of his golfing hobby, declared himself envious of Fulton Mackay's BBC television play *Going Gently*, a powerful study of two terminal cancer patients, in which Lancaster himself had attempted to interest the play-safe American networks. He was generous too in his praise of Peter Capaldi commenting: "He's a very funny boy with a genuine comic streak in addition to being a very good actor."

Riegert found the making of *Local Hero* a very special experience: "I'm proud to be around when there is this renaissance going on in the Scottish artistic family, as these people are really good. I'm not saying that to be polite, I really think this is competitively as good a set of people as any job I've done before and I've had a lot of good jobs. I think that's what's been so wonderful, to see that kind of real talent and enthusiasm for the various jobs, and mutual respect for what everyone is doing."

What then of Bill Forsyth, not that they had had first-hand experience of the man whose script had attracted them across the Atlantic in the first place? Lancaster, who finished work on the film before any of the others, had this to say: "It was a very difficult part for me to play but I feel pretty comfortable about it now because I've seen some of the results. Bill is one of the most original writers I've seen in a long time." Riegert was also firm in his conviction that, "Once people have the time and can look at what he's done he will be recognized as a great director. He is one of the best directors I've ever worked under."

Lancaster, a true professional, blended in well with the cast and crew, opposite with Bill Forsyth one of the most original writers he'd seen in years and this page with fellow veteran Fulton Mackay.

A lovely couple

Denis Lawson and Jenny Black

If the enormous international success of *Gregory's Girl* is to spin-off into the creation of a viable Scottish film industry then it will be the return home of working professionals like Denis Lawson and Jennifer Black that will signal its arrival. Both are Scots who have travelled to London to further their acting aspirations, and both regard *Local Hero* as an important job of work, taking great pleasure in the film's Scottishness.

The script of *Local Hero* called for the characters of village entrepreneur Gordon Urquhart and his wife Stella to be the most compatible couple in the world, and it was this very quality of compatibility which helped ensure that Lawson and Black were cast in the parts. However, it's not surprising they get on so well when their backgrounds reveal just how much they have in common.

Black, a striking brunette, was born in Glasgow and learnt her craft at the Royal Scottish Academy of Music and Drama, since when she has gained experience from a variety of roles in repertory and on television. Lawson trained in Glasgow and also worked steadily in rep throughout Britain and in television before his acclaimed 14 month run of *Pal Joey* in London's West End. For Jennifer Black her leading role in *Local Hero* represents her break into the world of cinema, for the slightly more experienced Lawson it is his most challenging cinema role as an actor following the anonymity of his work in *Star Wars* (1977), as well as parts in *The Man in the Iron Mask* (1977) and *Providence* (1977).

Although cast first, it was Lawson who faced a dilemma about his role. "I met Bill and we talked about

the film, then two days later I had an offer from the *Royal Shakespeare Company* to do a season with them. All my acting life all I have wanted is to be asked to work there, hence my dilemma. Anyway, my agent got me a script which I thought was wonderful. I needed to let the RSC know and said to Bill, look if you ask me I'll do it. I figured that the RSC will be there next year whereas a film like *Local Hero* won't, the film industry is very sparse. However, that's the business all over — either feast or famine." For Jennifer Black the dilemma stemmed not from whether she wanted the part, but whether the part was actually hers, as she explained: "Last November (1981) I had a phone call from my agent saying that Bill Forsyth was going to arrange to meet me, which he did. We met at a cafe in Glasgow, sat having tea for an hour and a half and he told me the story. I think I was probably one of the first people to see him, so he said he had lots more people to see and that was the last I heard of it until March when he asked to see me again. The funny thing was that up to that time I had not heard anything else about it, in fact I think at one point he didn't think I was quite right. I had to do a screen test and Denis came in to do it with me, he probably contributed a great deal to the fact that I got the part. We just got on well and Bill said, 'I think you'll make a lovely couple'."

As working actors the whole experience of *Local Hero* is part of a learning process that for the good actor never ends. Both agree that *Local Hero* has taught them much about film and the specific demands of the medium: "I am learning all the time," commented Jennifer Black: "The whole day is a process of learning, even technical things. I did not know what a focus puller did and things like that, and I've hung around a lot, asked questions and got to know things — that helps you appreciate what everyone else has to do — appreciate their problems,

Over: Denis Lawson and Jennifer Black are reluctantly awakened from early morning slumber to welcome Mac and Danny to Ferness.

Mac's 'Strictly business' attitude mellows as he discovers the finer things in life.

and when a technician asks you to do something you understand why." Lawson too reckons he has gained an insight into the craft of the cinema actor. "One of the things I wanted to learn was to act for the camera and how much to be aware of it when you are performing in front of it, how you position your body, your eyes and all of that. I made a mistake one day when we were filming in the church, the one day I felt nervy on the film. What I did was blow the scene in the morning and I forgot they would do a close-up in the afternoon. They did a broad shot and you kind of let things go as an actor and suddenly they were doing a close-up, and the scene was gone really, and I had a great deal of difficulty getting it back. So one of things I've learned to do is to pace yourself through the day and hold your concentration."

One way of learning is to watch the best in action, on *Local Hero* there was plenty of opportunity with the presence of one of the very best, Burt Lancaster. Jennifer Black remembered meeting the great man several years previously: "While I was still at Drama School going into my third year, I did *Antigone* at the Edinburgh Festival and he came to see it, that was about 1976. We were all excited and shouting in the dressing room that Burt Lancaster had been in the audience when suddenly this face appeared at the door saying, 'Do I hear my name being taken in vain?'. Funnily enough when we were on the West Coast at the Glenfinnan Hotel where Bill was staying one day, the register was lying open and Bill said, look at this, it said Burt Lancaster, it was 1976 and Bill said it must have been when he saw my new play." Lawson relished the prospect of working with Lancaster in the one scene they shared. "It was great. It was so funny, he was so controlled and we just fell about. There's a wonderful still of it. He's a delightful man. He wasn't remotely upset by it, but it was so crazy. You have this sense of the absurd because you are working with Burt Lancaster. We are eating oranges in this scene and had mouthfuls of oranges. My hands were dripping and I had to shake his hand. We just found it so absurd. The experience of working with someone like that, with his kind of knowledge of film was great."

Burt Lancaster remains disciplined and in control as all around him fall about laughing at the absurdity of the 'oranges' sequence.

If the film emulates the success of *Chariots of Fire* and *Gregory's Girl,* it would provide a showcase to the world for their talents, how did they react to the possibility of such success? Denis Lawson is understandably reticent: "I don't really think in those terms, when you've been working for a certain period of time in the business you become very realistic about things like this. The film comes out in the Spring, and I just hope that I will be working in an interesting way. I mean, don't get me wrong I want to be rich and famous, absolutely, I am very ambitious, but I also want to get better. I want to be a very good actor, so I hope the film is a success, but I am quite prepared for it to sink without trace." Jennifer Black, on the other hand, has no such fears: "I don't have any doubt that the film will be successful, no doubt at all. It will be wonderful and it will look so good. I told Bill that I could not understand how a telephone box with a sky behind it can look beautiful, but it does."

The impression is that a wide public acceptance of the film would just be the icing on the cake. *Local Hero* has been a very special experience in the working life of these two professional actors. Lawson summed it up for them when he said: "It's been wonderful. I'll miss it very much."

The script describes Gordon and Stella Urquhart as the most compatible couple in the world. Bill Forsyth felt Lawson and Black would make a lovely couple.

First steps
Peter Capaldi and Gordon Sinclair

The first thing that Peter Capaldi and Gordon Sinclair, two of the younger actors in *Local Hero*, have in common is that they are both Glaswegian and performers who started their careers in the city.

Whilst still at school, Gordon Sinclair became a member of the Glasgow Youth Theatre. Coincidentally, it was with this young company of actors that Forsyth made his first feature film, *That Sinking Feeling*, and in it a young Sinclair was part of a gang who raided a factory that makes stainless steel sinks. Out of his experience with Sinclair on that film Forsyth gave him the leading part of Gregory which really launched him in his film career.

Peter Capaldi was also pursuing creative activities before he was given the part in *Local Hero*. Capaldi was a student at Glasgow College of Art studying graphics. The college itself has, as its central building, a structure designed to the finest detail by Charles Rennie Mackintosh, a further testament that refutes the stereotypical view of Glasgow as a cultural wasteland in much the same way as the work of Bill Forsyth does. Capaldi was also a lead singer in a rock group called *The Dream Boys* at a time when Glasgow pop music and the, 'sound of young Scotland', dominated the London-based music press. Apart from being an entertaining interlude in his career this led to little further work for Capaldi, but

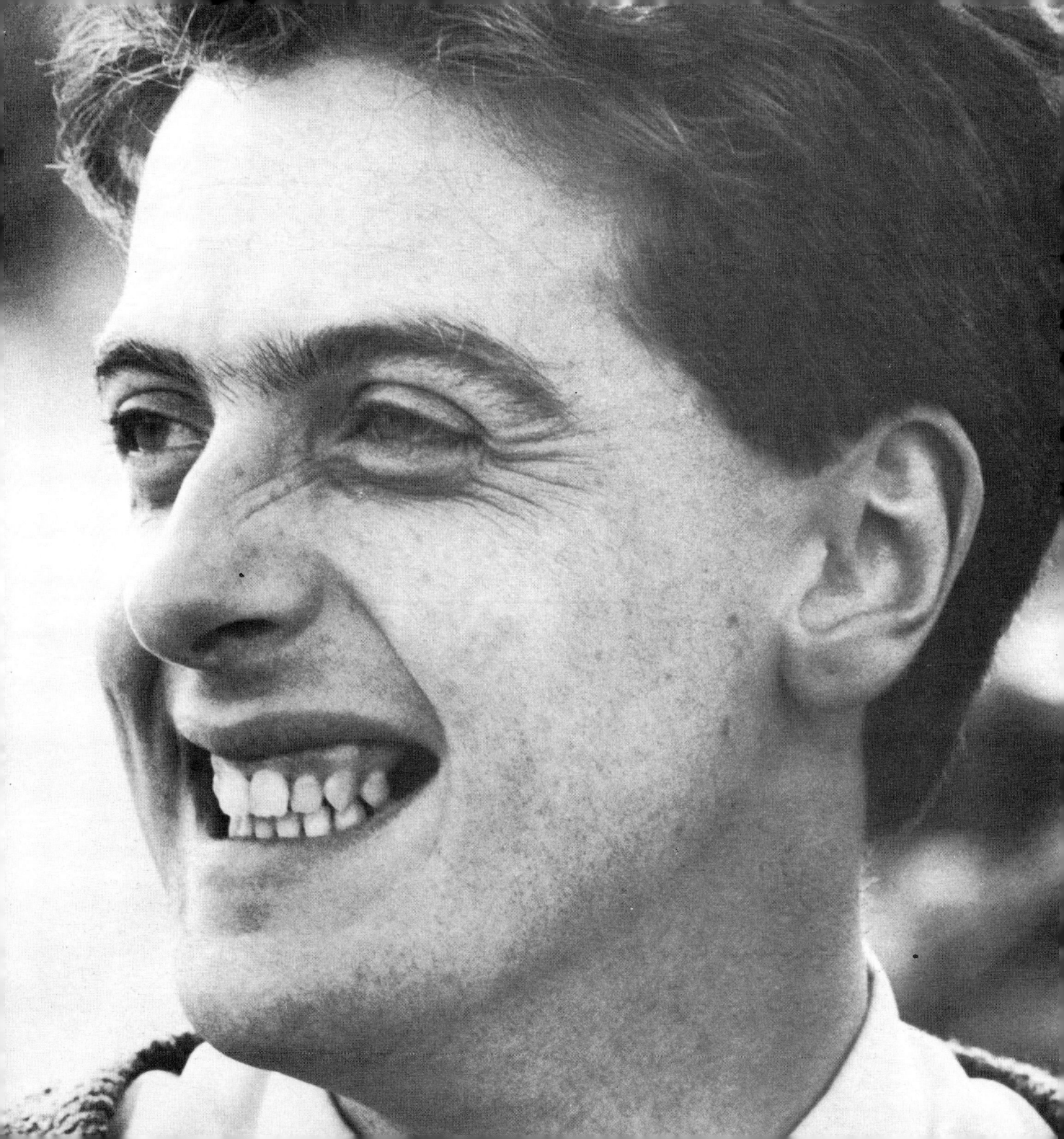

it did result in his trying his hand as a stand-up comic.

It so happened that Bill Forsyth knew the girl who lived in the same flat as Capaldi through her work on his BBC film *Andrina*. Thanks to this contact he came to see Capaldi as both rocker and comic. On one such occasion Forsyth arrived with an interesting proposition as Capaldi recalled: "This fellow who looks like a pixie with little sticky out ears came up to me and said, 'What are you doing next Summer?', I said I didn't know as I was unemployed, so he asked me if I would like to come and work on this film he was doing, of course I said yes."

Capaldi was told a little more about the film and found out that there was a ceilidh band in the story and assumed that he would be a member of the group, in other words just a small part. Suddenly he was to realise it was a leading part in a film to be produced by David Puttnam, starring Burt Lancaster and perhaps Henry Winkler. All that was pretty frightening as he admitted. In fact, Capaldi signed the contract only two weeks before filming began, having first gone through the whole technical side of securing a part including screen tests. Futile attempts to remain calm about the latter feature were not helped by his first ever flight on the 7 am shuttle from Glasgow before being whisked to Bray Studios, former home of Hammer horror films. He described the period as, "insecure and nerve wracking."

Bill Forsyth had been exceptionally successful in his casting of Gordon Sinclair in *Gregory's Girl,* and subsequently the young actor had gone on to complete his apprenticeship as an electrician before making a firm commitment to the acting world. Since *Gregory's Girl* he had played a small variety of other roles in a play and drama series for *Scottish Television* and a part in Lindsay Anderson's *Britannia Hospital*. Forsyth had indicated to Sinclair after *Gregory's Girl* that he would like to work with him again, and so when he was offered the part of Ricky, a cameo as the town tear-away, he was pleased to be working with his mentor again and neither surprised nor shocked not to be playing the lead. Sinclair had decided to be an actor and *Local Hero* was just more experience under his belt and hopefully a lot of fun.

Newcomer Peter Capaldi shares a scene and picks the brains of Peter Riegert and Burt Lancaster.

For Peter Capaldi it was a new experience and not always an easy or carefree one. To go from being on the dole to having a lead part in a major British film would be a jolt to anyone. Capaldi, an intelligent and thinking individual, didn't accept the life of a film actor without much consideration. "It's a kind of unnatural way of life — all this sitting around in hotels. People in this business, all they ever seem to talk about is food. I'm anxious to go back to some sort of real life." He explained that he felt it was quite an artificial lifestyle: "The real world is in such a horrible state it would be easy, even preferable, to sink yourself back into this fantasy world."

Another troubling feeling was that he was becoming too sensible. "I used to be far more fun than I am now, and another thing is that you talk about yourself all the time. You begin to think I must be one hell of an interesting guy when you're not, you're just like everyone else. It's weird, I feel ready to go back home, back to normal life." What is interesting about Capaldi in this respect, is that he was helping to articulate why, when an actor is interviewed or not acting he can often appear as if he were acting. It seems inevitable that in a profession where you are constantly thinking about how to portray emotions and images that an element of naturalness is removed. There were many more positive experiences for Capaldi however, in particular he was given the opportunity to learn his craft with a band of accomplished professionals, led by Burt Lancaster. "He made it very easy to work, obviously it's fairly daunting and frightening when you are confronted with this kind of legend. It was like a film. When I think back every time I saw him it was like a film I had sat through, but he did make it very easy. He grabbed me once and pulled me into his caravan to just go over lines which was quite heartening, because I was obviously nervous about doing lines with Burt Lancaster. He was great and he makes you feel at ease."

Gordon Sinclair's contribution to Local Hero, his third film with Bill Forsyth, is a cameo part as Ricky the town tear away. On this page he is captured during a quieter moment with Chris Asante.

Something that all the actors referred to when discussing Lancaster was the way he played to the camera. "It's interesting to watch to see the basic craftsmanship of how to hold yourself and how to move. It's funny when watching him do interviews; he becomes his on-screen self as soon as the camera comes on, then he pulls himself up more and throws his head over to a certain angle, all very craftily done, so it doesn't look obvious at all. I suppose after all these years of doing it, you get the hang of it," Capaldi observed.

Capaldi also worked closely with Peter Riegert. The building up of their on screen relationship proved interesting. Riegert was the first American Capaldi had ever known, and in a sense the relationship in the script of a small town Scot meeting an experienced oil executive was mirrored in the real life relationship, which initially existed between the two — experienced actor and green newcomer.

Capaldi believes he has learnt more from Riegert and Denis Lawson than from the mighty Burt Lancaster. "With Burt there's that big awe thing, and he was only with us for two weeks, so you can't get to know someone in that time, especially when he is a megastar. Peter Riegert's done so much stage work, quite a few films, and is very much into acting, he loves talking about it, and it's good that he'll put the effort into it. Peter was great about trying to calm me down and trying to help me deal with the technical problems."

After a nervous start especially during the screen-testing process where he was immensely reassured by the helpful Denis Lawson, Capaldi began to relax and enjoy a part with which he was naturally comfortable. "It's great being an idiot. Every time we did something silly, I watched the playbacks, and if I looked a total prat then I think it worked. Some days I come in and I think I'm fed up, I want to look cool, I want to wear my shades or something like that, but the feeling does not last long. You know there is something terrific when you can just admit you are a fool, or at least there is a big part of you which is a fool, and just let it out. It's really an exciting feeling to be so silly."

The combination of acting and effort which goes into the making of a film can be a very emotionally rewarding experience. Capaldi and Sinclair have clearly developed a strong affection for each other during the shooting and built up a durable friendship, having both gone through the same experience of a film debut with Bill Forsyth. They have also developed comparable feelings about other members of the cast and crew, in particular Denis Lawson. Gordon Sinclair felt that the party at the end of filming summed it all up. "Everybody was there in the one hall. I can't handle these situations, I just go to pieces and start bubbling. Denis Lawson was there, he gave Capaldi so much help. He's such a great wee guy, we got on really well with him. At the end of the party everyone was up dancing. I sat down, and Denis was at the table, I sat up at the other end deliberately or I was just going to start crying if he had said anything to me. So I then thought I should go and sit with him. He said, 'this is the time to talk', and I said oh Denis don't. It was the same after *Gregory's Girl*. They had arranged a barbecue, it's tragic in a way, you make friends and then they are taken away. It's so intense. Peter and I have since gone down to see wee Denis. It's good to cry."

Peter Capaldi went from being on the dole to film stardom and found the experience of working with the legendary Burt Lancaster more like a film than reality.

The Locals

One of the notable characteristics of Bill Forsyth's films, including *Local Hero*, is the creation of a community which surrounds the actions of the leading actors. In *Gregory's Girl* for example many of the small parts of teachers and pupils were given a chance to develop into defined characters, rather than be a collection of faces. This had two effects; the first was to provide a variety of amusing cameos and above all, to add to the general atmosphere of the setting.

This method of using a company of supporting actors was simple enough before *Local Hero* as Forsyth had the amateur members of the Glasgow Youth Theatre readily available. Nevertheless a collection of suitable Scottish actors was assembled by casting director Susie Figgis in tandem with Forsyth to play the villagers of Ferness. The concept was much appreciated by the actors themselves, as Tam Dean Burn who plays Roddy the barman remarked: "There's a lot of good small roles for Scottish actors instead of the usual four or five star parts and then into anonymity."

The use of a company of actors is an interesting concept and one often favoured by Hollywood directors of yore, like John Ford and Frank Capra. In Bill Forsyth's film the villagers of Ferness make up a particularly special mix of performers. Perhaps the best known is Fulton Mackay, a wonderfully accomplished character actor, whose more artistically notable stage performances in the Royal Shakespeare Company's *Nicholas Nickleby* and Ibsen's *Ghosts* and television work in *Going Gently* have been slightly overshadowed by the

enormous success of *Porridge*, the television sitcom in which he played, with a characteristic mixture of flair and precision, Mackay the prison officer.

Mackay is very much a product of the guts of the Scottish acting profession establishing himself initially as a working performer at the acclaimed Glasgow Citizens Theatre. Although he now lives in London, his Scottish identity remains strong. Disappointed at not being available for Forsyth's television film *Andrina*, he was delighted when offered the part of beachcomber Ben in *Local Hero*, and accepted the role without having seen a script. "I tend to be very chauvinistic about things like that. As he's a Scot, ready to burst out into a wider world, I'd love to go with him."

It so happened that when he actually received the script he was not particularly impressed, perhaps the only member of the cast to feel this way. "I thought it was too long, bordered on being fey, and I did not like the idea of the mermaid. I'd seen too many of these Scottish subjects treated in this way. I thought my part was good though, I recognised that." Annoyingly Forsyth tended to agree. "It was like George Bernard Shaw taking the bow after a successful first night and one man in the audience booed and he said, 'I agree with you sir but who are we to disagree with so many'. Bill kind of said that with me in *Local Hero*. I agree with you, I've got grave doubts, you know how he talks, but *they* all think it's quite good."

Mackay had actually worked with Forsyth before. Whilst working as a documentary film-maker, Forsyth started his own company called Tree Productions and Mackay spoke the commentary on a film about Scottish forests. "I had good memories of Bill Forsyth of that time but I had not associated Bill Forsyth of yore with the director of *Gregory's Girl*. It was only when I was doing *Britannia Hospital* that he came on location and reintroduced himself."

Despite misgivings about the script Mackay enjoyed the experience of making *Local Hero* along with the majority of his colleagues. "Bill was charming. He had

This page: Fulton Mackay emerges from Ben's shack.
Opposite: villagers David Mowat, Ian Stewart and Willie Joss.

great humility and yet there was a mind always at work filmically, I trusted that absolutely and found I could really act for him in a way I'd almost forgotten. I had said to Bill that I believed in classical acting, by that I meant reducing things to essences and just being very simple. He said who would be an example of that. I said Spencer Tracy and he said O.K., he knew what I was talking about. I could be more naturalistic and then select from that in a way that was not entirely naturalistic and which pleased me. With Bill I really felt free to act, what I did would not be rejected and indeed I could go further and do anything with the part and he would add or subtract from that."

Ray Jeffries, who plays the town drunk Andrew, is also a product of Scottish entertainment, if in a rather different way. He paid his dues through the cabaret circuit throughout Scotland, working alongside such names as Rikki Fulton. Ray Jeffries is, in the nicest possible way larger than life, the sort of guy who is the life and soul of a party and can always find a crack the morning after, when everyone else is suffering quietly from the previous evening's excesses. *Local Hero* is his first film actually made for the cinema, although he does have a variety of television experience behind him. His pleasure at being in the film was obvious and clearly genuine: "I was so excited about working with Burt Lancaster, come on let's face it, he was one of my childhood heroes. I suppose it's like getting a new toy for Christmas when the guy comes up and speaks to you." As far as Ray's children were concerned: "They couldn't give a damn about Burt Lancaster. They want a photo of me with Gordon Sinclair because they thought he was great when I took them to *Gregory's Girl*. When they're my age they'll probably say it's great to see John Gordon Sinclair as an old man playing the *Birdman of Alcatraz*."

Edith Ruddick, whose part is simply that of an old lady, took the same sort of route as Fulton Mackay — RADA and for a while the Citizen's in Glasgow. However, the pressures of a family led to her giving up full time acting and she began teaching drama instead. *Local Hero* was, in a sense, a comeback for her and an experience made all the more enjoyable by the presence of Bill Forsyth. "I was absolutely charmed that he had offered me the part because I had seen and admired his work and his attitude and I would have stood on my head to please him." This, incidentally was not required. However, Ruddick had plenty of opportunities to observe Forsyth at work with the company. "I think he used the company to create the authentic feel of the Scottish scene and to create little crystals of information about these people. I think of the two old men Willie Joss and Ian Stewart burbling on forever more, or the two men in the pub, Charles Kearney and James Kennedy, the way he created the punk character around Caroline Guthrie. Then, in the harbour scene when the guy comes off the Russian trawler there's Caroline, Anne Scott Jones, Sandra Voe and myself being paid tribute to. Bill's talent for picking the right people is very highly developed."

One very important lady within the community of Ferness is oceanographer Marina whose status as a mermaid may be in doubt, but whose role as spiritual defender of the bay is undisputed. She is played by Jenny Seagrove, who could be forgiven for thinking 1982 had been designated as her year. Early on in the year her big break in television came with a leading role in the BBC serial of Wilkie Collins' *The Woman in White*, before *Local Hero* she picked up a degree of film experience with the small role as Jereny Irons' wife Anna in *Moonlighting* and made a short film *A Shocking Accident* based on a Graham Greene story. Immediately after *Local Hero* she went to film in the South Pacific, co-starring opposite American actors Tommy Lee Jones and Michael O'Keefe in the big-budget high seas adventure *Savage Islands*. Quite a year for an arresting young actress whose original ambition was to be a vet. "I got the requisite number of 'A' levels to go to university and learn to chop up animals," she says, "Then I thought, 'I can't stand blood, or needles and I can't do it,' I decided then that I wanted to be an actress. I'd always done little plays, written my own and played the leads in school plays."

Born in Kuala Lumpur, Malaysia, Jenny claims to regret the network of roots a solid English upbringing would have brought but values the confidence and independence a travelling youth gave her. Her acting aspirations took her to the Bristol Old Vic Theatre School where

Jenny Seagrove added to her successful run of 1982 film and television discovery as oceanographer Marina.

she spent three years and has since worked in theatres around the country and in television staples like *Crown Court* before the exposure of *Woman in White*. The role of super-intelligent marine researcher Marina who doesn't appear to suffer fools gladly was a challenge. "Marina is an elusive character. I did some research at the Institute of Oceanography to discover what somebody who has five degrees might be like. Somebody that bright would be totally obsessed — obsessed by the sea and her marine biology. She's terribly intelligent, self-possessed and mischievous. I think she's enchanted by Oldsen because he's so naive and innocent, not at all like the kind of man she normally meets. He's the total opposite of her and she's distracted by him." She had originally envisaged Marina as a cross between Bo Derek in *'10'* and Ursula Andress in *Doctor No*. Given the Scottish weather conditions this wasn't exactly how things turned out: "No make-up, a blue-nose, blue fingers and feet, tatty hair! Mind you, it's very good for me because I'm beginning to be stuck in the role of pretty young things. It is nice to do something which isn't that." Jenny remains equally level headed about her discovery this year by the media: "I think the media are quite desperately looking for a new face. If it's me then I'm delighted, but I'm kept down to earth at home because I live with somebody totally sane. In this business where you get is a matter not particularly of talent but of circumstance, luck and whether your face fits. Then you have to prove you've got it, come up with the goods when the opportunity presents itself. Success is so ephemeral, you're somebody one week and forgotten the next. It's important to keep a perspective on it."

Apart from the Scottish actors there were two non-Celtic villagers. Chris Asante plays the part of the black minister, a rather different challenge from his role in the film of Frederick Forsyth's novel *The Dogs of War*, (1980). Above all this African born actor had to acquire the dreaded Edinburgh Morningside accent made

Ben emerges from the village shop surrounded by talk of the Americans money deals. Opposite: David Mowat and Peter Capaldi discuss the mysteries of mermaids.

famous in *The Prime of Miss Jean Brodie*, as he felt that the character would have undoubtedly attended Edinburgh University.

Chris Rozycki had different problems. Rozycki is Polish and he had the task of speaking English in a Russian accent for his part as Russian trawler skipper Victor. Rozycki left Poland in the late seventies to join his mother who had lived in England for ten years, leaving not just his birthplace, but also a considerably successful acting career. In Britain his problems with English were initially to hamper him, but once this hurdle was overcome work began to flow and only recently he appeared in Warren Beatty's *Reds* (1981).

As Forsyth had hoped the company of about 20 actors worked together very successfully. There seems to have been many good reasons for this, chief among them the fact that they were all solid professionals. As so much of the shooting of the film was completed on

location for long periods of time the company did actually have to live together. Edith Ruddick certainly saw the effect of this forced cohabitation. "In Fort William our hotel was miles out of town and by the nature of the hours we worked together and all that sort of thing we were more or less pushed into each other's pockets for company quite a lot of the time — just the same as a village. Bill knew what he was doing in getting us all together all of the time." It was certainly not something that worked out by chance, as Forsyth explained: "It was intentional and I would have liked to have made more use of it, because I know it's something that Peter Riegert found a tremendous benefit. Living with all the other Scottish actors, he was in the village that was in the film because he was drinking with them and eating with them and so in the few scenes he had the sense of knowing them as if he had been living with them for a while, which is the situation in the film. So in that way it worked." Indeed over the filming a kind of mutual appreciation developed between Riegert and the company as he explained: "They are really talented people. I can't tell you how easy it is to do a scene with a group of them because they are so strong. You scrap like hell over each scene. I look in their eyes and they're saying come on." Members of the company were equally complimentary of Riegert's open nature. Ray Jeffries said, "Peter Riegert's been great. He has friends like Robert De Niro and tells us stories about him, and we tell him about Scotland and Rikki Fulton, and he's genuinely interested. He's saying if you're ever in New York, let me know and we'll have a party. I canny manage a week in Dunoon."

Despite the apparent pleasure which seems to have been derived by members of this well-paid company Bill Forsyth was unhappy that he was unable to use the company more than he did. One of the problems was the

Chris Asante perfects his 'Jean Brodie' accent during a scene with Denis Lawson.

Opposite: Ray Jeffries (right) strikes a characteristic pose during filming in Pennan.

length of the script which was about 150 pages long. "I think I cheated with the company a bit, I gave them the feeling that there would be a lot of opportunities for improvisation. I thought there would be, but once we started there was so much script that it was a struggle to get through that without having too many chances to build other things into it, so I knew other people felt a little frustrated that they were being used in a kind of background way. I was very aware and very conscious that every chance I had to give them things to do, I would. It comes out very well in the film because they all have a sense of being real characters."

It is one of the achievements of *Local Hero* that a community has been created that can stand comparison with the band of characters in the 1948 Ealing classic, *Whisky Galore*. In that film Gordon Jackson played one of the villagers and if one considers the success he's had since then who know what may happen for some of the performers gaining their big screen break as the villagers of Ferness.

David Puttnam

David Puttnam has been a significant force in the British film industry almost since the time he entered the business in 1969. Paradoxically over the 14 years of his involvement Puttnam has flourished whilst the cinema-going audience has dwindled and indigenous production has hiccupped along, never quite as terminal a patient as prophets of doom have made out, but hardly rosy in health either. In this context *Chariots of Fire* became more than a flim, it carried part of the hopes for the quality British film industry that might be. Puttnam himself has very definite reasons why he's in the film business. "I'm in the film business for a very simple reason," he says. "I want to make people feel the way that films made me feel when I first started going to the cinema. That's where the conscious decision to try and get into the film industry came from when I was 10, 11, 12 years old. The first film I ever remember seeing was *Pinocchio* (1940) and I came out of that thinking it would be an amazing thing to do with your life."

Born in 1941 in London, the son of a photographer, and educated at Michenden Grammar School he enjoyed a successful career in advertising before his entry into the cinema. The success of films like *Bugsy Malone* (1976), *The Duellists* (1977), *Midnight Express* (1978) and *Chariots of Fire* (1981) and his ability to grant cinematic life to directors more accustomed to working in commercials, has provided a useful label to classify a varied career and one of which he is understandably wary. "It's very dangerous to segment anyone's life. One does things for a series of reasons that are not

necessarily what they appear from the outside. I started off working with directors who came out of television, because they were the sort of directors I wanted to work with. Then, as much by luck as by judgement, I was able to work with Alan Parker who wrote the very first film I ever did and we managed to get him off the ground as a director. Because I managed to get some interest in him I was then able to work with Ridley Scott who I'd also known for years, but you must remember during this time I also worked with Michael Apted twice, and with Marcel Ophuls, who was a documentary director, a man called Philippe Mora who'd been a painter and now, funnily enough, if you look at all the films I'm working on at the moment, there's one with Apted which I've just finished, there's Gavin Millar who's an ex-critic at the BBC, Roland Joffe who's ex-BBC and Bill. All your life is a series of drifts. I think a sensitive person, God knows I hope I'm sensitive, is aware of the fact that they're drifting slightly to the left or slightly to the right in textural terms. If you're sensitive and sensible you try and correct that. That's what I've tried to do with this film. At the same time there is a type of film I've admired for years that I've never made, which is a film like *Battle of Algiers* (1966) and my great hero is Francesco Rosi. I've never made that type of film so again I think I'm trying to trim and alter slightly in that direction and I hope that the next picture I do after *Local Hero, The Killing Fields*, will be the furthest I've gone in that direction. *Midnight Express* had elements of that, but it also had a heavy theatrical layer."

Local Hero is however distinguishable from his more recent ventures for several reasons mostly connected with Bill Forsyth. Forsyth is both a writer and director, with two film hits to his credit and an unfussy technical style born of his work in the documentary field. The latter was something Puttnam welcomed: "Yes it is different in the sense I felt I was in danger of making films where style was swamping content. I quite consciously wanted to make a film where the content swamped the style. Quite deliberate, and that was one of the things with Bill. I mean that's why I didn't push or encourage him into having a very stylish art director or a very stylish cameraman. I felt he should have people who would put on the screen something simple."

Chariots of Fire was style personified, and whilst a tremendous personal triumph unfortunately served to foster the cult of personality intent on establishing the name of Puttnam as synonymous with that of the British film industry, a claim which is of course exaggerated. Other people produce British films; people like Don Boyd, Mark Shivas, Handmade Films and the team of Clive Parsons and Davina Belling who made *Gregory's Girl*. Puttnam is an optimist and inspires fellow-workers with his enthusiasm. However, he is also a realist and unlikely to let his heart rule his head. An attempt to establish a documentary tradition in the 1970s with films like *Brother, Can You Spare a Dime* (1974) and *Double-Headed Eagle* (1973) was quietly shelved on the discovery that there just wasn't an audience to support it. He is also keenly aware that for every film he makes, two or three other projects will fall by the wayside and when the final product doesn't live up to expectations he is the first to express reservations, as in the case of *Foxes* (1979). However, producers don't win Oscars without good reason, and David Puttnam obviously has particular film-making strengths. Co-workers assert that there is a special magic about a Puttnam film, a magic which is formed by the attitude of the man at the top, David Puttnam. Hugh Hudson, director of *Chariots of Fire* has called him one of the best before and after men in the business citing his expertise in setting up a project, lack of interference whilst filming and promotional activities afterwards as evidence. Jonathan Benson, assistant director on *Chariots* and *Local Hero* had this to say: "David has a more human attitude than any other producer I know, he covers every aspect and is clued up on all of them. He doesn't show this side but he loves a confrontation, a fight or a struggle, it taxes him a bit. There is an immense loyalty towards him and a family atmosphere on his films. He's not high up, but accessible to everyone and makes one feel like an exceptionally important person to the making of the film. He has a tentacle in all known pies but I don't think he personally makes a lot of money from his films. He is

David Puttnam confers with Bill Forsyth on his first big-screen project since the Oscar-winning Chariots of Fire.

the only producer I know who gives a percentage to the crew and I must have worked on 40 films. He won the Oscar, but it belongs to all of us."

It was the award-winning success of *Chariots of Fire* which gave Puttnam the financial go ahead to begin *Local Hero*. The idea for the film had its origins in his dissatisfaction with the state of screen comedy, as he explained: "I don't like the sort of comedy that's been prevalent, it's not the type of comedy that really makes me laugh. I find the Pythons amusing, at times really very funny. I love, for example, *Ripping Yarns*. I thought they were marvellous, I really think they were terrific; better than any of the movies. I liked *Blazing Saddles* (1974), since then I haven't really liked Mel Brooks films. I haven't been a great fan of the American knockabout style, it hasn't got to me. On the other hand I've always been an immense fan of the Capra and Sturges pictures which I think are genuinely funny, a different sort of humour. So I was trying I suppose to climb on the back of whatever Bill had to offer, to try and persuade him to make that kind of film."

Given the subject matter of the film what parallels did he then see with the humour of Capra and particularly Billy Wilder whose films, *Love in the Afternoon* (1957) and *Avanti* (1972) depicted the blossoming of Americans abroad? "Well, I think there's a certain classicism in taking anybody out of their natural environment into another environment and seeing how they swim. It's always good for a laugh, it's an interesting area of humour which maybe isn't done enough. *Ninotchka* for example, Wilder did it a lot — *Sabrina* (1954). When you go through the hardcore of what we see as quintessential American cinema you find very few native-born Americans. There's no more American films than the Capra films, yet he wasn't actually American, not really and neither was Wilder or Lubitsch, and maybe it explains the reason they had that tongue-in-cheek look at their society. Bill had a remarkable quality of a huge affection for Scotland and an amazing objectivity about Scotland. He is as Scots as you can get, yet he is extraordinary, he talks about the Scots sometimes as if he's talking about someone else."

On paper the partnership of Puttnam a dynamic, voluble man and Forsyth the retiring Scot seems an unlikely one, how did Puttnam feel it had worked out? "I can only tell you how it works from my point of view and he would have to give you the reverse thing. I'm not sure what I give Bill and wouldn't be presumptuous enough to say so. In terms of what he gives me, I find him an absolutely reliable man, sometimes taciturn so that you're a little unsure as to where you're going or what you're doing. On the other hand he's always come through. I've grown to trust him more and more not less and less, sometimes it goes the other way. I trust his instincts, that's the most important thing. What I like is that he allows me a bit of room to do my job well. He's not an easy person to work with because he's not verbal; the easiest people to work with are people who you can sit down with and verbalise the problems, agree them and walk away from them. Bill, I think, likes to leave stuff on the table and I think probably in his terms rightly so. I think maybe Iain and I were a little unresponsive to his need for room, on the other hand we all created problems by not cutting the script enough and didn't give ourselves the room. However, I know we both have the same dreams — that's crucial." Forsyth is equally appreciative of Puttnam's role in the film. "He's been great. Really supportive. I've only worked with real producers twice. I was really apprehensive with Clive and Davina because they were from London and big time people and that worked out well. Again with David, he was very successful and I was very apprehensive. However, it's been a delight to find out how good producers can be. He's made enough films now to know what a producer should be in his own terms. We did not have a lot of problems. It would have been interesting to have had a couple of big problems to see how we would have got on. I know now that we got on famously and it's been a really good relationship. When you are involved in a project there is a chance of becoming a little blinkered, so what the producer does is act as devil's advocate. It's his job to question almost every decision you make, just to make sure you are making it properly and to give you something to bounce off. It also gives

Puttnam with his star Burt Lancaster who together with Bill Forsyth were all award winners on the night of the British Academy Awards when the total budget for Local Hero was finally secured.

the director the chance to see whether he is really serious about something because if there is an objection to an idea then if you really believe in it you'll see it through, if not you'll back off. It clears your own head in a funny sort of way."

Puttnam hopes that the fruits of their collaboration will provide audiences with an experience that only cinema-going can offer. "It seems to me people walk into a dark cinema, it's a very important fact that it's dark, because they wish to experience something which is not happening outside. They don't go in to observe, that's my point. I don't believe people walk into cinemas to observe, they can watch television to observe, they go into cinemas to experience and there's not much point experiencing something unless in some way it moves you. It can make you laugh, cry, not really think but definitely feel." *Chariots of Fire* exemplified that theory to perfection, and the instincts which pulled Puttnam towards that material repaid him handsomely. What then were his predictions for *Local Hero*? He was typically enthusiastic: "I think we'll get great reviews and we'll have to fight for an audience like we had to with *Chariots*. I'm very sanguine, I think we could have a big hit and, in fact, if I had a million dollars to invest in a film, and I was having to look at *Chariots* and at *Local Hero*, I actually would put my million dollars on *Local Hero* at this point. I think what I'm really saying is that if it's a very big success it will be less of a surprise to me than *Chariots*. I think it's a film like *Chariots,* the same quality in one respect, it's a film I think the public's waiting for. The public is there, they don't know they're waiting for it but I think there is a real sense this sort of film is in the air. I've always known it was going to be a good film, recently it moved into the area of maybe it's a great film, with cuts and trims and changes we've made. I think we've now got three or four things we did that I think have made an immense difference to the picture. I am now buzzing with excitement over it. I love it. I absolutely love the film. Let's put it this way — it's a ship I'm prepared to go down with."

David Puttnam with Bill Forsyth the man he hopes will provide a film where the content swamps the style.

Bill Forsyth

Four years ago Bill Forsyth was almost unknown outside the closed world of the film industry. Yet the making of *Local Hero* received unparalleled coverage in the media, for in the eyes of the opinion-forming press Forsyth had arrived. This was partly the result of the critical and financial success of *Gregory's Girl* and the potential that was shown in *That Sinking Feeling*. It was also the fact that Forsyth was Scottish and his sudden pre-eminence was further emphasised by his appearance from a largely moribund indigenous film industry.

However, while to many people this was the classic case of overnight success, Forsyth had more than paid his dues in the business. The son of a plumber he joined a local film company as soon as he left school in Glasgow. "That was in the old days of the one-man documentary film companies. One man and a boy, and I was the boy. We made sponsored films and documentaries. Unfortunately this apprentice way of entering the industry doesn't happen very often now."

Working as a camera assistant and assistant editor for five years he then went to the National Film School, after which he returned to Glasgow and formed a documentary and sponsored film company, which survived the next six years making some three or four 16mm short films a year. As Forsyth says: "It was virtually a hand to mouth existence. Money is the perennial problem in the film industry, simply because making films is an expensive business." *That Sinking Feeling* was made literally on a shoestring budget and

Forsyth recalls, "I don't remember the film being much fun, we were so short of time and money." Yet, the film was made and from it came the more secure finance for *Gregory's Girl*.

The obvious question asked about any suddenly successful man is what is he like? It is difficult enough for any close acquaintance to know what a person is really like let alone a journalist on the basis of interviews. Yet two different forms of evidence can help in describing a person. On the one hand you have his relationships with other people, how he treats them, what he is like to work with and so on. Also you have the evidence of his work which can amplify certain characteristics. The problem is illustrated by the following impressions. Chris Menges told us: "This is a really modest man finding his way. He's about learning. He wants to know about things." Peter Riegert hailed him as "One of the two best directors I've ever worked under." David Puttnam was of the opinion that, "his particular strength is not as a film-maker. I think his particular strength is as a communicator. I think he's got a very, very wonderful vision of people. Not so much life as people. Bill has a unique ability to feel out the best in people and he has an innate belief in the best of people. He's a remarkably uncorrupted and unsoured man." Fulton Mackay describes Bill as, "charming, what I liked about Bill was that he was almost undetectable from behind the camera and then he would come forward with just a little note and dodge back again." Forsyth himself disarmingly claimed: "I'm not really a very good director in a technical sense."

Despite all these opinions a number of characteristics do stand out. Talking to those connected with the film it was obvious that Forsyth was liked, admired and respected beyond the call of mere politeness and duty. His popularity is based on real affection.

Forsyth comes across as shy, even diffident yet with the charm he undeniably has, there is an inner self confidence and even obstinate belief in himself. Chris Menges offers an insight into this part of his character.

Forsyth provides the implicit direction observed by performers Peter Riegert and Peter Capaldi.

"Bill had an interesting way of dealing with the money side of the shooting. Time and time again people would come up and say, 'we are overshooting' or, 'the script is too long' and Bill would say yes I agree and do nothing about it. He's the most stubborn director I've ever met. Usually when a director is told this they quiver in their shoes and change, they don't let you know but they change! Bill would agree with everything that was said but do nothing." This characteristic is often the result of a person knowing what he wants. Menges described, with thoughtful insight, what motivates Bill. "Bill is not scared of where he is and recognizes *Gregory's Girl* was O.K., he's really pleased it made money, and is quite happy to take money from David to make his new film because he sees himself as learning, he's really interested and just wants to know more. Just like a kid is supposed to come out of school, so Bill just wants to find out what this world is about. Many film people don't think in that way, they think of ambition, conquering their souls, of great drama, fame or the great acclaim of life. Bill's not about that."

Forsyth's three feature films do tell us something about what he is about. He is a Scot and proud of it. "I am very fond of my country. I've become more so recently the more I've become aware of it. It's a delight to be able to present it to people on film, well this is us, or that's what I think we are." In all his films many Scottish elements are presented with affection; whether it's the football in *Gregory's Girl*, the need for brain transplants amongst the populace in Paisley in *That Sinking Feeling* or Scotland's two favourite drinks — whisky and iron bru. Denis Lawson particularly appreciated Forsyth's portrayal of a contemporary Scot in the screenplay for *Local Hero*. "He writes Scottish parts that are very direct and very modern. This character I'm playing, what's nice about him is that he's a modern Scotsman. He's not some stereotype. He's bright, attractive and even sexy as well. All the things which are normally not in Scots parts."

Forsyth is often compared with Ken Loach, the excellent politically orientated English film director whose films are noted for their social realism and political honesty. Forsyth's style is different but he cares nonetheless. *That Sinking Feeling* is about a robbery set up by a gang of unemployed teenagers, and whilst the project is outrageously funny and far-fetched the 'message' is there. Forsyth himself says: "There's always something you want to say. I would not want to make a film that did not say anything, I'm not interested in getting into something that just a piece of entertainment, a James Bond or an adventure film. I don't enjoy filming that much, in fact I don't enjoy filming at all and to go through all that for the sake of money would just not interest me." In this context a major project like *Local Hero* was not embarked upon lightly and Forsyth sees a number of influences at work. "I saw it along the lines of a Scottish Beverly Hillbillies — what would happen to a small community when it suddenly became immensely rich — that was the germ of the idea and the story built itself from there. It seemed to contain a similar theme to *Brigadoon* (1954), which also involved some Americans coming over to Scotland, becoming part of a small community, being changed by the experience and affecting the place in their own way. I feel close in spirit to the Powell and Pressburger feeling, the idea of trying to present a cosmic viewpoint to people, but through the most ordinary things. And because both this film and *I Know Where I'm Going* (1945) are set in Scotland, I've felt from the beginning that we're walking the same... treading the same water."

The single most noted characteristic of Forsyth's work is humour. His humour is very recognisably Glaswegian yet the parallels with Woody Allen seem the most obvious. Forsyth is sympathetic to the comparison: "I think that Glaswegian humour is very similar to New York humour, which is really Jewish humour for it is the humour of despair, the humour of the gallows. The humour of awful circumstances or predicaments. I think that is where humour comes from. From situations where the only way out is to laugh, for survival's sake. At the bottom of every joke is a piece of despair, you can't produce a laugh without it. If someone falls on a banana skin you get a laugh, but someone gets hurt."

There is also another comparison that can be made with Allen and that is a similar attitude to love. In both *Gregory's Girl* and *Local Hero* Forsyth presents the ideal or perfect woman. In the new film Marina, the mermaid and Stella are both highly desirable, and yet mermaids don't exist and Stella is faithfully married to someone else. As with Dorothea in *Gregory's Girl* the ideal is largely unobtainable. As in the same way Woody Allen creates the character of a girl he either cannot

Forsyth finds the technical side of film-making arduous but accepts the challenge of widening his experience on Local Hero.

have or is unable to keep. Without drawing anything out which is too profound, both Gordon Sinclair as Gregory and Peter Capaldi in *Local Hero* believe that their characters are based on Bill, whilst Allen plays the insecure, paranoid lover himself.

There are three elements of importance in discussing Forsyth as a writer-director; his script-writing, his casting and his direction. Forsyth explained why he began writing: "I'm only a writer because at a certain stage in the making of a film you have to write. I'm only a writer in the sense that it's part of making a film nowadays. Even with *Gregory's Girl* I asked a number of writers, and for various reasons they said no, so I had to write it myself. And so that is how I got into writing." As to whether it was difficult, "If you don't think about it, it's not difficult. Like everything else, if you think about it too much you fall off. I've just learnt one thing, you get to know yourself and how you work. I know I'm very lazy and if I push myself I don't get anywhere. I've just got to take time, and so I spend a lot of time not doing anything. I delude myself into thinking I'm not working and that makes me happy because then I know things are happening in my brain and I spend about six months not writing — taking notes, thinking things and just structuring things on bits of paper, not actually sitting down and writing. I think that's the secret, not sitting down at the typewriter too early. All in all it was really only two months in front of the typewriter and many months of thinking about it." As if to highlight the way Forsyth needs a long gestation period his next project *Singles* has been at the back of his mind since 1973. The malt in this case is just about ready for public consumption.

One of the notable features of the Forsyth way is casting, the way he chooses actors has a special relevance to his method of direction. "In terms of the way I work it's about 80% of the work I do. I spend a lot of time on it. Probably because I don't think I'm a very good director. It's one of the safety things I do, I pick very good people and I pick people who are really the

characters before I start out. I think I take a lot of care with casting because it's easier when I'm filming. Only once or twice in quite a lot of filming have I been forced to coax a performance out of someone on the set. The way I manage to work is to get the characters and performers there before I start filming." Apart from the practical reasons for his casting methods Forsyth does have an enviable ability to talent spot. Gordon Sinclair and Clare Grogan from *Gregory's Girl* have made a great impact since that film and were just about unknowns before that, while in *Local Hero* Peter Capaldi and the Jennifers Seagrove and Black seem set to make a comparable impression.

Also within Forsyth's casting are the roots of his directing style on set. When filming he keeps a very low profile. Edith Ruddick described his style as implicit rather than explicit and she is right in the sense that the actors know exactly what is required of them and Forsyth gives only the occasional word of guidance when required.

When someone is built up as quickly as Bill Forsyth has been then he faces the danger that his flavour of the month status will wear off. "People want heroes," Fulton Mackay told us with a sigh. "I think it's unfair and dangerous, He has done one really successful film. He's at a stage where things are opening up and he's doing a bigger subject with a star in it and he's had to go to America. That must be quite traumatic for him. I hope it's a great success for him because I want him to build on what he's already done, but it's a long road to hoe. I think his films show he is innocent, I would say it is his greatest talent. I would do anything for him, even if *Local Hero* was awful and we have got to allow that making a film nicely does not mean it's going to be a good film."

In the end Forsyth can only do what he thinks best with a hope that the critics and public will respond to what he offers. *Local Hero*, if nothing else, has been another lesson in the continuing education of Bill Forsyth film-maker. He has learned the usefulness or otherwise of the video playback, about the length of scripts and leaving room for improvisation; *Local Hero* was 150 pages long, he claims that will never happen again and that his ideal length is around 90 pages. He also hopes that the film will tell film-makers something about his aspirations. "I hope it will let certain people see that I have my limitations in what I want to do. Now due to my success, people just assume that I want to be a successful film-maker so my agent gets a lot of, 'when is he coming over to America and will he do *Stars Wars 4*' and all of that. When I went over to America it was quite boring and ended with me being quite rude. People saying when are you coming to the States as if it was everyone's ambition. After a week I got quite short with people who asked me that. I asked them when they were coming to Glasgow. If Robert Altman finds it difficult to make films in America I'm not going to try. He's a hundred times better film-maker than me and if he can't get away with it there is no way I'm going to try."

If Bill Forsyth was to be seduced by success he would not be the first, so many British directors have left home for the seductive American dollar, and yet Forsyth seems the most unlikely candidate. A story underlines the qualities of the man; after the premiere screening of *That Sinking Feeling* at the Edinburgh Film Festival in 1979, the film met with a more than favourable response. The critics, ever ready with advice for a new champion, were quick to warn Forsyth not to be changed by success and to keep his feet firmly on the ground maintaining the truth and integrity of his work. Forsyth could be forgiven for accepting this wisdom with a wry smile, in the 24 hours prior to the film's screening, when economics dictated the role of the self-publicist, he could be found scurrying around the city arranging posters and displays to inform the good public of Edinburgh of his new adolescent epic. Hardly the behaviour of a man likely to be dictated to by money or success.

The part of Felix Happer was written specifically for Burt Lancaster and Bill Forsyth was delighted when he agreed to appear.

Appreciation

Local Hero is, as Bill Forsyth admits a strange film, a lyrical, poetic work tinged with an aura of melancholy and sadness. For a director most noted for his comic world Forsyth is tackling some serious themes here, isolation, love, friendship and money.

The central character of Mac is shown as a hollow embodiment of the American Dream, a whizz-kid businessman with a plush apartment, living a successful life who has never questioned the how and why of his being. In Houston he enjoys material wealth but the quality of his life is dubious, he lacks friends and lavishes his affections on a sports car instead. The effect of Ferness on this subconsciously dissatisfied man is profound. Here he sees the support and structure of a true community and observes first-hand the warm and tender loving relationship in bed and business enjoyed by Stella and Gordon Urquhart. The village may be sited on the edge of the world, cut off from civilisation but Mac is far more isolated from warm humanity in the bustling centre of big city USA. He changes, and this most materialistic of individuals is suddenly willing to give up his car and well-paid job for the camaraderie of the village. He is seduced by the notion of escaping the inhumanity of the urban sprawl for the all enveloping beauty of life in the Highlands. The last scene of Mac back in his high rise home staring at the shells from Ferness beach is a powerful reminder of what might have been.

The villagers however are not paragons of virtue but subject to human weakness and not immune to the lure of great wealth. The normally even-keeled tempo of Ferness life is thrown widely askance by the arousal of avarice when Mac arrives. The villagers even consider dispatching Ben when he seems the only remaining obstacle to their collective gain. However, the philosophy in the film is that people are generally worthwhile and if they stray from the path of goodness events and characters are redeemable. Ben's stubbornness saves the villagers from themselves, bringing research and study to enhance the area not, 'development' to despoil it. Mac is made aware of the shallowness of what his life has meant, and even Happer can be himself, a man who wants his head in the clouds, nearer to the stars and not bored with the minutiae of power.

Local Hero is a film of many strengths but one without stars. The only real star is Forsyth himself whose vision of humanity is the film's *raison d'etre*. It is acted with a pleasant ensemble feeling, although the villagers tend towards attractive wallpaper. The film lacks the intensive focus of one character's travails as in *Gregory's Girl* choosing instead a diversity of emphasis. Fulton Mackay grasps a strong opportunity in the character of Ben for a brightly etched portrayal of simplicity and wisdom and there is a strong visual sense to the piece. Chris Menges' breathtaking photography more than justify's one recent claim in the British Film Institute's Monthly Film Bulletin that he is, 'the most exciting cameraman working in Britain today, as well as the most versatile.'

Local Hero is the product of a developing talent rather than the mature artist yet it marks a progression for Forsyth and an important pointer for the future. Undoubtedly some of the audience which watched and enjoyed the lightheartedness of *Gregory's Girl* will be lost on this very different film. For the sake of Bill Forsyth, truly one of the nice guys in the business we can only hope that the film will find an audience, and contribute to keeping alive the very special experience of going to the cinema.

The credits

HAPPER	BURT LANCASTER
MAC	PETER RIEGERT
BEN	FULTON MACKAY
URQUHART	DENIS LAWSON
MORITZ	NORMAN CHANCER
OLDSEN	PETER CAPALDI
GEDDES	RIKKI FULTON
WATT	ALEX NORTON
MARINA	JENNY SEAGROVE
STELLA	JENNIFER BLACK
VICTOR	CHRISTOPHER ROZYCKI
REV MACPHERSON	CHRISTOPHER ASANTE
CAL	JOHN JACKSON
DONALDSON	DAN AMMERMAN
RODDY	TAM DEAN BURN
BABY	LUKE COULTER
MRS WYATT	KAREN DOUGLAS
SKIPPER	KENNY IRELAND
FOUNTAIN	HARLAN JORDAN
PETER	CHARLES KEARNEY
SWITCHBOARD OPERATOR	BETTY MACEY
GIDEON	DAVID MOWAT
ANDERSON	JOHN POLAND
ACE TONE	BRIAN ROWAN
LINDA FRASER	ANNE SCOTT JONES
MR BULLOCH	IAN STEWART
RUSSIAN GIRL	TANYA TICKTIN
JONATHAN	JONATHAN WATSON

ACE TONE	MARK WINCHESTER
FRASER	DAVID ANDERSON
ACE TONE	ALAN CLARK
ACE TONE	ALAN DARBY
PAULINE	CAROLINE GUTHRIE
ANDREW	RAY JEFFRIES
SANDY	WILLIE JOSS
EDWARD	JAMES KENNEDY
SWITCHBOARD OPERATOR	MICHELE McCAREL
ACE TONE	RODDY MURRAY
CRABBE	BUDDY QUAID
OLD LADY	EDITH RUDDICK
RICKY	JOHN GORDON SINCLAIR
SWITCHBOARD OPERATOR	ANNE THOMPSON
MRS FRASER	SANDRA VOE
ACE TONE	DALE WINCHESTER
IAIN	JIMMY YUILL

WRITER/DIRECTOR	BILL FORSYTH
PRODUCER	DAVID PUTTNAM
ASSOCIATE PRODUCER	IAIN SMITH
LIGHTING CAMERMAN	CHRIS MENGES
MUSIC	MARK KNOPFLER
EDITOR	MICHAEL BRADSELL
PRODUCTION DESIGNER	ROGER MURRAY LEACH

U.K. PRODUCTION MANAGER	ROBIN DOUET
U.S. PRODUCTION MANAGER	PAT CHURCHILL
FIRST ASSISTANT DIRECTOR	JONATHAN BENSON
ASSISTANT DIRECTORS	MELVIN LIND
	MATTHEW BINNS
	JOEL TUBER (U.S.)
PRODUCTION ACCOUNTANT	RON PHIPPS
ASSISTANT ACCOUNTANTS	MAGGIE PHELAN
	LOUISE COULTER
LOCATION MANAGERS	DAVID BROWN
	DENNIS BISHOP (U.S.)
PRODUCTION SECRETARY	MARY RICHARDS
PRODUCER'S SECRETARIES	LYNDA SMITH
	DIANE CHITTELL (U.S.)
DIRECTOR'S SECRETARY	TERESA COLMAN
CASTING	SUSIE FIGGIS
	PENNY PERRY (U.S.)
CAMERA OPERATOR	MIKE COULTER
FOCUS PULLER	JAN PESTER
CLAPPER LOADER	JAMES AINSLIE
CAMERA GRIP	KEN ATHERFOLD
CONTINUITY	PAT RAMBAUT
	ANNE RAPP (U.S.)
SOUND MIXER	LOUIS KRAMER
BOOM OPERATOR	MIKE TUCKER
SOUND ASSISTANT	ALLAN BRERETON
ART DIRECTORS	ADRIENNE ATKINSON
	FRANK WALSH
	IAN WATSON

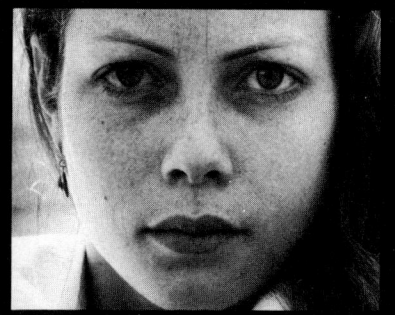

DUBBING EDITOR	IAN FULLER
FIRST ASSISTANT EDITOR	JIM HOWE
SECOND ASSISTANT EDITOR	ANNE SOPEL
ASSISTING DUBBING EDITOR	DAVID GRIMSDALE
UNIT PUBLICIST	SUSAN D'ARCY
UNIT STILLSMAN	GRAHAM ATTWOOD
PRODUCTION BUYER	JILL QUERTIER
MODELLER	STEVE SIMMONDS
PROPERTY MASTER	ARTHUR WICKS
DRESSING PROPS	GEORGE MALIN
	TED STICKLEY
DRAPE	ALEC HEARN
PROPS	BILL STARK
	JOHN HOGAN
SPECIAL EFFECTS	WALLY VEEVERS
	PETER HUTCHINSON
	PETER SKEHAN
	PATRICK McCOLGAN
	STUART GALLOWAY
	ROY CARNELL
COSTUMES	PENNY ROSE
	PIP NEWBERRY
MAKE-UP SUPERVISOR	TOMMIE MANDERSON
MAKE-UP ASSSISTANT	KAREN DAWSON
HAIRDRESSER	BARBARA SUTTON
CONSTRUCTION MANAGER	RON EVENS
CHARGEHAND CARPENTER	STEVE ALLAWAY
CARPENTERS	ROY HANSFORD
	DENNIS BOVINGTON
	ANTHONY ALLAWAY

STAND BY CARPENTER	MARTIN HAMMERTON
CHARGEHAND RIGGER	LEAS BEAVER
SPECIAL EFFECTS RIGGERS	TOMMY PARKER
	DENNIS HARRISON
STAND BY RIGGER	GEORGE HOBBS
CHARGEHAND PAINTER	TED RESTALL
PAINTER	JOHN HURLEY
STAND BY PAINTER	NORMAN NORTH
STAGEHAND	BARRY GATES
STANDBY STAGEHAND	EAMONN REDMOND
PLASTERERS	DAVID COLDHAM
	RAY STAPLES
GAFFER ELECTRICIAN	RONNIE RAMPTON
CHARGEHAND ELECTRICIAN	BRIAN MARTIN
ELECTRICIANS	RON LYONS
	JOHN BEACH
	MICKY WILSON
	MICKY DAVEY
RUNNERS	GUS MACLEAN
	CHARLES FINCH
NATIONAL FILM SCHOOL ATTACHMENT	IAIN BROWN
LOCATION CATERING	J & J FOODS

GRAPHICS BY JOHN GORMAN
TITLES AND OPTICALS BY G.S.E. LIMITED
COLOUR BY KAY LABORATORIES   LONDON LIAISON JOHN HEMMING
MPAA NUMBER 26894

Filmography

Bill Forsyth, the writer-director, has previously filmed two of his screenplays **That Sinking Feeling** (1979) and **Gregory's Girl** (1980). A former documentary film-maker he has also made **Andrina** for the BBC based on the short story by George Mackay Brown. Winner of the 1981 BAFTA Award for Best Screenplay he is a member of the recently formed Scottish Film Production Fund Committee. His current project is a small-scale film **Singles**.

David Puttnam, the producer, has been involved in a varied number of productions since entering the world of films in the late 1960s. His credits include **Melody** (1971), **The Pied Piper** (1972), **Swastika** (1973), **Double-Headed Eagle** (1974), **That'll Be The Day** (1973), **Mahler** (1974), **Stardust** (1974), **Lisztomania** (1975), **James Dean — the First American Teenager** (1975), **Brother, Can You Spare a Dime?** (1975), **Bugsy Malone** (1976), **The Duellists** (1977), **Midnight Express** (1978), **Foxes** (1979) and **Chariots of Fire** (1981) for which he won the Oscar. A member of many influential film industry bodies he has contributed to Channel 4 through the 'First Love' series of films for television and has two film projects in preparation for 1983: **The Killing Fields** and **Body Line**.

Burt Lancaster who stars as Felix Happer is a former circus acrobat who has appeared in many critical and commercial hits since his film debut in **The Killers** in 1946. His best known films are **Sorry, Wrong Number** (1948), **The Flame and the Arrow** (1950), **The Crimson Pirate** (1952), **Come Back Little Sheba** (1952), **From Here to Eternity** (1953), **Apache** (1954), **Vera Cruz** (1954), **Rose Tattoo** (1955), **The Rainmaker** (1956), **Sweet Smell of Success** (1957), **Gunfight at the O.K. Corrall** (1957), **Birdman of Alcatraz** (1962), **The Leopard** (1962), **Seven Days in May** (1964), **The Train** (1965), **The Professionals** (1966), **The Swimmer** (1967), **Airport** (1969), **Moses** (1975), **Twilight's Last Gleaming** (1976) and **Atlantic City** (1980). An Oscar winner for **Elmer Gantry** (1960) he has directed two films; **The Kentuckian** (1955) and **The Midnight Man** (1974). Since **Local Hero** he has filmed **The Osterman Weekend** for director Sam Peckinpah.

Acknowledgements

The authors would like to thank the following people and groups for their assistance in the writing of this book; David Puttnam and Iain Smith at Enigma for saying yes to the idea in the first place, Bill Forsyth and the entire cast and crew of **Local Hero** for their time and consideration both during and after filming, Teresa Colman for her unfailing courtesy and helpfulness and stillsman Graham Attwood whose pictorial record of the production adorn's the book's pages.

The following people deserve our gratitude; the staff and students of Polygon Books especially Neville Moir, Vicky Taylor, Murdo McDonald, Andrea Joyce and Bill Spence, our designer Charles Miller and Marie without whose support and encouragement the enjoyment of writing this book would have been singularly less.

Allan Hunter & Mark Astaire